Dear Jan + Marie : 9/15/07

The Eye of an Angel

by
Ashley Underwood

"Enjoy the Book"

Ashley Under—

authorHOUSE™

1663 LIBERTY DRIVE, SUITE 200
BLOOMINGTON, INDIANA 47403
(800) 839-8640
WWW.AUTHORHOUSE.COM

First published by AuthorHouse 2/28/2006
ISBN: 1-4208-0882-6 (sc)
ISBN: 1-4208-0881-8 (dj)

Printed in the United States of America
Bloomington, Indiana

This book is printed on acid-free paper.

Author Note

The identity of the characters, who figure in the story doctors, nurses, and other hospitals personnel; patients and patients' families; and friends, places have been changed,certain situations disguised, to perserve the privacy of the one's involved.

Three doctors names' in this book I could name and I am greatful to each of them .

Dr. Gregory Cunningham, Dr. Scott Eisenberg, Dr. Mehmet C. Oz.

I haven taken some research material from the liberties. But the stories in this book are true. Every experience recorder material here happened.

And I am so greatful for everyone who assisted me in making this book possible, I owe special thanks to the Authorhouse. To my friends and families who were there for me that nurtured this book every step of the way. To those I love I dedicate this book.

Ashley Underwood.

Acknowledgement

Cheryl Rushell Butterfield, Editor

Arlene S. Uslander, Editor

Larry Le'Von Butterfield Sr.

Larry Le'Von Butterfield Jr.

George Butterfield Jr.

Dr. Gregory Cunningham M.D.

John Cunningham, MA

James E. Cunningham

Dr. Scott Eisenberg M.D.

Dr. Mehmet C. Oz, M.D.

Mary Magovern, RN

Carolyn Zagury, RN, PhD

This Book Is Dedicated:

To my Jesus, "The Eye of An Angel".

My lovely dream husband, Le'Von
Who married me and made my dream come true.

Daughter Cheryl Rushell, who encouraged me to tell this story,

JR. son, who gave me his strength to keep pushing and finished it.

With love to my father, the late John B. Cunningham,

to my late mother, Ethel L. Lynn Cunningham.

My late sister-in-law and best friend, Dolores Mary Butterfield,
Thomas, Lovely words, "Don't give anyone something you don't
have."

And my late brother, Richard M. Cunningham: lovely, kind words
still live on in my heart. "Never give up. Keep smiling.
You can do it."

Contents

Introduction

From the depth of her heart and soul to you, and yours, I am

pleased to take you on a

Journey you will remember in years to come:

"The Eye of An Angel."

This book is about a woman struggling to find peace with her inner

voice and soul.

She took the risk to expand to her full potential as a writer,

going into the deepest places in her soul.

Within her heart, both pain and passion lie, which is only

accessible when she

faced her fears and "The Eye of An Angel."

This book contains pictures, stories, of near-death experiences,

and research education.

It reveals dreams that will lift up your heart and sharpen

your knowledge. It will make you think.

You will have a different outlook on life itself.

You will find miracles, love, hope, faith, and encouragement in

these inspirational stories.

It will make you laugh and it will make you cry.

This book is a beacon in times of confusion and challenges.

It will comfort you in times of need.

I believe you are about to take on a lovely experience.

Jesus has been good and I must share my story

so you, too, will find the faith to believe in miracles.

The Eye of An Angel

From Day One

*S*omething was wrong. Her husband had to leave the hospital to go back to run the family business, but already she had an uncanny feeling, like there were a million crazed butterflies dancing inside her stomach. She would be alone for the rest of the day – alone on what would be the day of her most frightening day of her life. Thoughts of death began to sneak into her mind. These thoughts had been pushed into the back of her brain. Why were they popping up now?

It was the afternoon of June 8, 1972. Danielle had entered the hospital to undergo emergency fibroid surgery. As a thirty-two year-old mother of two, who was otherwise in good health, she had chosen to follow her doctor's advice to have the operation. Her husband, Napoleon, and she were comfortable with the decision.

And now, Danielle still felt comfortable with the decision, but something else was gnawing on her mind now – something she couldn't quite put her finger on.

During the seven years of their marriage, Danielle and Napoleon had rarely spent a night apart. And now, alone in the cold, sterile hospital room, she tried to reflect on their family and the special closeness they enjoyed. The young couple had two children; a six-year-old daughter and a four-year-old son. Danielle and Napoleon were reluctant to leave them with the baby sitter. Even on their "Special Nights" (date nights), they were all together.

Sometimes, on these "Special Nights," when their daughter was twelve and their son ten, they would make dinner for Danielle and Napoleon. They cooked a special dinner and did the entire trimming and serving in the family room. The children would put on a CD from their collection, and it was usually just the right one -- maybe not the one Danielle would have chosen, but perfect, nevertheless. Danielle recalled the day when her daughter made her special dish of creamed spinach, baked chicken, and blackberry wine served in Danielle's crystal wedding glasses. Afterward, the children washed the dishes and then we'd all retire to the family room to watch TV-DVD.

They turned the lights down low and the reflections of the fire were so relaxing, they fell asleep before the movie was ever over. Danielle seemed to have finally found some peace on earth.

As Danielle looked back on the past, she realized how lucky she was to have two beautiful and healthy children and a wonderful husband as considerate as Napoleon. He had taken the following day off to be with her after surgery, and planned to spend a few days at home while she recuperated.

He and their two children were already making plans for our families annual July 4th, cookout and pool party. But, a feeling of foreboding settled more heavily upon her. Danielle thought it was the darkness she had learned to dread as a little child, or maybe these silly feelings came from another experience, an experience that toke place in her childhood home years ago, which still spooked her out.

When Danielle was three years old, her father used to go to work at four o'clock in the morning. Back in those days, her mother had to get up very early in the morning to make her father a hardy breakfast. As the fifth child in a family of ten children, Danielle hardly knew what time her dad went to work, or came home. Her mother went to live with Danielle's grandfather when her grandmother died and Danielle's dad stayed with the children down on the river near his family. At that time, three of the children, including Danielle, were in school.

In April, just two weeks before Easter Sunday, Danielle developed a strange rash over her entire body. She shared a full-sized bed with her older sister, and when she began to shiver uncontrollably, Danielle remembered leaving her bed one night and getting into her sister Dee's small bed. Danielle was crying because of her fever and because she wanted her mother. When her father came home from work that night, he discovered that she was out of her bed. He took her back to her bed, which was damp and wet with perspiration. Dee tried to tell their father that Danielle was sick, but he didn't listen to her. And finally, on the second day, Danielle was taken to the doctor, and her family was given the bad news. Danielle had Rubella Measles, and there was nothing anyone could do. 'They would just have to wait it out', the doctor told Danielle's father, 'and he should contact Danielle's mother right away'.

Danielle remembered the doctor saying that if she made it through the next forty-eight hours, she would be out of the woods. Danielle was thinking to herself, *'But I'm not in the woods'.* She seemed to slip in and out of sleep. Once, Danielle felt hands on her head, and looking up, she saw her mother leaning over her and softly crying. Her Mama had given Danielle some red oak tea and packed collard green leaves around her neck. She'd said that would draw the fever out of Danielle's body. Two of her older siblings had died years before from childhood diseases, so Danielle's mother was willing to try just about anything to save her child from that same failure disease. "Oh, she is just a baby. It can't be happening again," she said as her eyes filled up with tears. "Please, Lord, don't let this happen again."

Danielle heard those words and drifted back to her feverish sleep again. She snuggled further down into the covers and felt warm and content. Her mother's words gave her hope, and she closed her eyes to sleep again.

Danielle awoke to her mother's stressed voice. "Too late to take her back to the doctor. I think we've lost her, John B." Then in a whisper, "Our baby is dead."

Danielle felt the cover pulled up over her head. She thought her mother was just trying to keep her head warm. What did she mean, "It is too late"? She turned over on her side and looked around her room. Danielle noticed it was filled with what seemed like hundreds of men and women, all dressed in white standing by her bed. And Danielle remembered thinking, "I'm like a small fly in a large bowl of buttermilk." Then the men and women walked away and Danielle became aware of another person nearby. Suddenly, she was not lying in bed, but found herself underneath a big bird wing. Danielle looked and saw a woman with a beautiful floppy white feather looking down at her. The feather fascinated her. It seemed whiter than white, with a sparkling bright light that seemed to come from within. Danielle felt perfectly calm and peaceful with the woman. She sang softly and cradled Danielle under her wings, and although Danielle did not know who she was, Danielle did not want to leave her.

"She's breathing again." Her mother and father came running into her room. But, it was a different room. Danielle was moved into a smaller room that was very dark. The woman with the white, fluffy wings looked like her dead grandma and then she was gone. Danielle's little body was wet from perspiration and she was frightened. Her mother turned the light on; they had taken her back to the doctor's office. When the doctor arrived, he told Danielle's parents that they were very lucky. The child had made it. Danielle heard the words, but they did not make sense. How could she have been lucky when she was so sick? When she awakened, she asked her parents who the strange woman was, and they said they had no idea what she was talking about.

Danielle told them how she had heard what they said about her being very lucky to be alive, and how a woman with the sparkling light in her feather had come and held her, but they had no answers. They never did. This experience would be Danielle's to cherish as a gracious showering of love throughout her young life. The memory has never changed, and each time Danielle remembers it, she has a sense of calmness and happiness. She felt so safe under the wings of this person.

Danielle recalled that feeling now as darkness seeped into her hospital room. Ever since she was a child, the darkness had terrified her. Now, alone in the darkness again, a strange feeling was in her bedroom. Death seemed to be creeping all around her. Her thoughts became filled with it, caught up in it. Death and the High Power gave His only forgotten son and that seemed eternally, forever. But, what awaited Danielle on the other side? She thought to herself, *'If I were to die today or tomorrow, what would I find? Is death eternal with a vengeful High-Power?'*

Danielle was not sure, and it was not what she had learned as a child in Sunday school. She could still remember every detail of the first school building with its brick walls and its dark, cold room. The school didn't even have a lunchroom -- only a thick cardboard that separated the junior-high students' classrooms. Danielle still remembered when her sister was sent to another classroom that ran along the perimeter of the school. They were separate from each other and although the distance was small, it felt like they were in another world, away from home all day. Danielle still could remember that first morning when her older sister had to fight a large boy for her younger sister, and the fear in her eyes as she fought to get off the ground. Danielle thought her heart would break. Her two sisters and she was taken to a small room where the teachers lined each one up against the wall, and one by one were placed in chairs and each of them had to wear an identification tag around their necks for the next four years in school. Danielle's older sister, Annie, was separated from her and her other sister, and sent to another room for older kids. That first day, Nancy and Danielle would line up with the other girls and were marched into the room where they stood by their chairs until the teacher told them to sit down. Then they promptly started to recite, "I pledge allegiance to the flag of the United States of America…"

The lights were turned down and the front doors were left wide open for the light to shine inside. This big, overcrowded room with the dark wall horrified Danielle, and she waited in terror until it was time for lunch.

On Sunday, they all attended church, which offered Danielle and her siblings a chance to visit with all their cousins. It was like a family reunion. As Danielle fought through the crush of folks to get a hug from her grandfather every first Sunday, she felt a peck on the head. She turned around and saw a large fan her mother used to keep the children in line in church, and this would be the first of many times Danielle felt it. She found it difficult to understand what the problem was and why she had to go in front of the church and sit on the mourning bench, kneel and pray, and they were not allowed to look back while they were in church. But, Danielle was able to see her friends and this was worth any punishment from the fan.

The children were taught about God at an early age, and Danielle learned many things she had never considered. She was told, for example, that if they told a lie, or did anything wrong, they were sinners, and, of course, she believed that. Her mother was the chosen one in the High Power's eyes, and they learned that their mother was there to guide and protect them. Danielle was often spanked by her mother with a small branch from a tree and was then forced to get down on her knees and ask the High Power to please forgive her. Danielle believed, and began to fear the High Power immensely because of her church-school teaching. Everything she learned about Him intensified this fear. He seemed very angry and impatient and very powerful, which meant that He would probably destroy her, or slap her straight into hell, and before she died on Judgment Day, her body would not get cold. The High Power was a being she hoped never to meet.

*****

Danielle looked at the clock on the table. Only minutes had gone by since Napoleon had left – only minutes. The dim bulb at the entrance of her room produced only enough light to cause dark shadows that hung in her imagination of nightmares from her past. Her mind must be racing, she thought, propelled by her loneliness -- racing through the dirty, dark corridors of her memories. Danielle had to control her fears in order to find peace or the night would be endless. She finally settled herself, and thoughts from her past again entered her mind.

A light bulb went off: community college. She would never forget reading on her first day at the college office: "Equal Opportunity for all." She had thought, of course, that this sign referred to all colors and people. She was there to be trained to become a registered nurse.

Nursing school proved to be a more positive experience than her earlier one. She enjoyed the professional atmosphere, and the teachers seemed to enjoy their students and appreciated being around them. Danielle learned that the High Power meant different things to different folks, instead of the angry vengeful High Power she had thought He was before, these people taught her of happiness – a High Power who was pleased when they were happy. These devotional folks often shouted, "Thanks,' Big Brother.'"

It took a while to get used to their sudden outbursts. Danielle recognized that there were different ways to view Big Brother and to worship Him. She thought she remained convinced that He was

6

still the Big Brother who would punish her when she died and stood before Him.

*****

Danielle joined the Baptist church at the age of eleven and was baptized in an outdoor pool. Many folks witnessed it. She attended church almost every Sunday and when she attended, it did not seem as important as the fact that her curiosity about Big Brother grew. As she matured, she realized that He was playing a major role in her life. She just wasn't sure what that role was or how it would affect her as she grew older. She approached Him in prayer to get answers, but Danielle did not feel that He liked her. Her words just seemed to dissipate in the air.

When Danielle turned eight years old, she was very curious about Big Brother, but she would not question her mother or father. She did not want them to know she had not learned it from Sunday school. Danielle told herself she would try to find out from her Sunday school teacher.

Danielle thought of all the ways she could ask her and finally she just asked the teacher in front of all the kids, "Do you believe there is a living God?" Danielle thought the teacher would explain it to her, but you would have thought she had said a bad word, and by the time the teacher finished talking to her, Danielle just wanted to vanish -- she felt so small. All the kids were in a state of shock.

Danielle prayed that the teacher would not tell her mother. She felt that she would go to "reviver" (In the south they had a revival meeting at church for five days at nights once a year, during which they had to spend a lot of time on their knees praying for forgiveness.) She was certain that she had made a complete fool of herself; however, now Danielle knew that she was doomed to hell, and nothing was going to stop her from going there, because she had no faith and because she had questioned the existence of Big Brother. Danielle was sure now that she would be with the devil forever.

Later that summer, Danielle started back to work full-time and she had an experience that paralyzed her with fear. One night after taking a bubble bath, she was lying out on the patio gazing at the stars, the moon and passing clouds. Danielle often thought about her

7

older brother and sister who had died at a young age, and her little twin brothers, floating around in heaven in the clouds.

Something Danielle had enjoyed at an early age many times before was when her brother and she would see who could count the most falling stars and make a wish before the stars hit the ground.

Suddenly, her eyes caught a ray of white light coming down from a cloud, and Danielle was spellbound with fear. The light moved from side to side as if it were playing a game with her. She thought that this was her dead grandmother coming to take her away and she screamed at the top of her lungs.

Danielle had been informed several times that when family members died, God sent another one back to replace them. Her father ran out of the house and looked all around. He reassured her that no one was there, but it took a while to calm her down.

Danielle continued to search for the living God, as she read every single page in her little black Bible looking for the truth. She had believed that when a person died, his spirit would be outside his grave and his body would remain in the grave, but he would come back as an animal until Jesus came again. Then, when Jesus came back, he would sound his trumpet and the dead would wake up. Danielle thought of this often and wondered what it would be like to have crossed over, and left all of her love ones.

The Man In Her Dream

Danielle's vision was that she wanted a tall, lean, strong, cameral color, nice-looking man with wavy or curly hair, light brown eyes, strong hands, integrity, and spiritual truth, with a sense of security and knowledge of making money and having money. Danielle wanted someone who took pride in himself— someone loving, happy, and who respected and cared about other people. Would tonight be the night she would see his tiger-colored eyes, and he would steal her breath, and she would fall in love? Eagerly, she waited in the darkness, blinded by the light of the moon. "Come to me," she whispered, "in this hour and on this night" The longer she waited, the more her soul craved a taste of his lips. She wanted him to hold her in his strong arms, to taste his tongue, to feed on the love deep down in his soul.

As she lay there trying to sleep, she said, "Take her heart. It's yours to keep." As the darkness came all around her, she waited alone for the love of her life that she desired.

Why couldn't she fall asleep? The moonlight had disappeared in the darkness of the clouds, and the stars had gone away. As she lay there, she felt herself drifting, floating down into the darkness. There, the green-gold, bright-white silver lights made her slip into a deep sleep at last.

As she was running through the woods, on a bright, hot summer day, she felt as though her heart were in her throat, beating rapidly. She lie down under this large oak tree, near the water and regroup. The light of the twilight sunshine was in her eyes, as she lay there daydreaming about what she wanted to be when she grew up and lived in a great big house.

It was no wonder then that Danielle fell hopelessly in love with the young man in her dream. When she was fifteen years old, she had a dream about meeting this gorgeous man, falling in love at first sight and marrying him. As she lay in her bed, counting the falling stars, she made a wish, and when she finally fell asleep, she had a dream about being in this large park, sitting alone by the lake, daydreaming and listening to the blue jays sing. In her dream, she glanced out of the corner of her left eye at this shadow from behind. She jumped up to run and fell back into those powerful, arms.

9

His eyes met hers, and he said, "I am sorry. I hope I did not frighten you." Danielle said it was all right. She knew from that moment one day, she was going to marry him. The next morning, her mother awakened Danielle. She dashed out of bed and yelled "Mama, Dee, she had a dream. It was so vivid, and she was going to make it happen after Danielle graduate from high school".

Danielle finished school in May and she worked and save enough money to move to New Jersey. She was on a mission, and it was very hot in the Deep South in August that year as Danielle was packing her bags the sweat was poring off of her body as if she had took a shower. There family members took Dee and her to the bus station. It took them about three days before they arrived in New Jersey.

A friend of the family met them at the bus station and the first thing Danielle noticed was that the folk seem very cold and unfriendly. Dee had told her the folks in the Northern States were unlike the folks in the Southern States, African American folks were so difference and they would not speak to you even if you were looking right down their throat They walked around like the world owed them a living. Danielle fined that hard to believe So one day Dee and her was walking cross town and they meet these African American, Danielle decided to test them out and as they approached them she said "hello, it a nice day out today" Well they looked at her "saying I know she not talking to us" and the two of them started to laugh as they ran down the street.

The African American and the white folks they all seem alike here they were not as friendly as the folks back home .

The folks back home would at lease say good morning, wave to you driving down the road, or they would tip there hat if they had a hat on. The white folks seem friendly and if they did not like you. They would let you know that too, and at lease you could see the bullet coming. But, some of the folks in the North they will smile in your face and shoot you in the back. The same can be said about some of the African American folks. Danielle also founded folks in the Southern and Central Jersey the majority was color coded. Where as the Northern Jersey folk was different and easy to work and talked too and they respect each other rights and less color coded

Danielle felt that she did not come all this way to make friends, but if she did she would be grateful, but if not she could always talk with her sister Dee at lease they had each other, Danielle felt that if she had decided not to take this journey, or even tried to follow her dream she would always wonder the "what if or may be". Danielle felt she wanted to leave the past in the past and she is looking to the future and that are not yet born. But tomorrow's is beyond our immediate control. Only one thing we know for sure is that the sun will rise in the east and set in the west.

Danielle felt she can fight the problems just for one day, and because all of though yesterday's, and not knowing what to expect tomorrow can drive a person crazy. She believe living for today and tomorrow will take care of it's self.

Danielle had a plan she believe taking one day at a time and keep the faith and determination. She believes in keeping her vision clear and following her dream, wherever it may leads her.

One day when Danielle dad took her to the store to get a new pair shoes and she wanted a pair of brown high tops strain up's with hookers on them. Danielle feet were to big her dad looked at her and said you are becoming a big girl now and you have to wear big girl's shoes. Danielle looked at her dad and said but, Dad you don't understand.

"Danielle said, you see dad she don't want to grow up". Danielle founded it hard to make the transition from childhood to adolescence, this dream reveal the conflict she was facing at the time. Danielle still remember in her adolescents years she was still playing with her jacks and rag dolls, and having make believe boyfriends and she felt very comfortable in that mode.

Danielle felt after a while her journey became easy and that she could have never image in her wilder dream this would be the most awesome journey she would take and the most comfortable one she could ever dream of.

Danielle believes that all things are possible, if you believe and she remember reading that when she was just a young child in Sunday school. Danielle fined that when she feels down she remember those words they encourage her to keep to the plan.

11

She would say this too will pass and nothing stays the same forever.

Danielle felt as an adult her dreams marked her transition into puberty and pointed to the discovery of her creative power down from the lower world. In her dreams she could face her conquered and her fears through the power of the light and make a descent to find herself within her subconscious.

Danielle felt that her dream was a milestone in a psychological sense as well as a biological process. She felt that if she recognition and celebrated her dream it might ease the crisis of adolescence and bring to light the psychological feeling necessary to embraced her growth.

She believes in dreams and pays closed attention to them, weather it a culture thing or the peak of a transformational cycle or a ripe opportunity in life when change is forced or maturation such as adolescence. She believes there is some true to your dreams. One thing Danielle remembered when she was walking down the street in Jersey she noticed a lot of horses and buggies, and there were a lot of Nuns, with there habits on there heads. She immediately felt that she wanted to be one too. Danielle remember telling her sister that she want to be a Nun because they all seen very happy and pleasant to talk with. She remembers her sister asking her what about this man in your dream? Danielle told her she still wants to marry him too. Dee said if you become a Nun you will not be able to many a man too. Danielle said she just though it would be nice. It reminds me of the olden days Mother talked about when she was growing up. Some folks riding horses and buggies and some were walking around with all this black on. Dee what going on here? Well Danielle "I tried to tell you but you did not believe me". Dee what going on? Danielle this is part of there religion. Danielle said "Old my God"

"Old my God" she was feeling sorrow for them and she though one of there family members had crossed. Dee thanks you for reminding me about my dream man and she stuck to her plan. One late September afternoon Danielle came home from work and she was thinking about her High school boyfriend she has left back home and she was about to turn another leaf over in her life. Danielle remembers feeling a natural high. She was somewhat surprised when she did not feel any fear or sadness that seemed warranted in her situation. Instead she just bouncing around likes a basketball girl after winning one of her basketballs games. She was smiling and infinite patience with her sister. She was washing dishes in the sink and drying them and placing each one in its own special place, like she had no care in the world.

Danielle felt all of a sudden this strange, elated feeling came over her she believed this was the peace within her, and let go of the feeling that was holding her back from her dream.

Danielle was just standing there looking out of the kitchen window day dreaming and all of a sudden she spotted this tall, lean, caramel-skinned handsome man walking down the street with two girls on each arm. Danielle, "Oh, no; she thought. This cannot be happening to her" "she sees him" she said.

Yelled No, "Oh no"

. This is the man she saw in her dream.

"What is this suppose to be"? His two angels one under each arm or is the Devil try to steal her joy? Danielle yelled to her sister Dee, this is him do you believe this Dee, this is him——-

Dee said, "You see who?"

Mr. Nick "You see him? Mr. Nick asked, "See who"? Danielle the man that was in her dream, Dee 'the man that was in your dream" Danielle? Yeah, Dee looked out to see this dream man and her eyes flying wide open. "It does look like the man you told Mom and I about".

Danielle told her sister and her land-law "this is the man she going to marry" Dee asked what about the two girls in his arms? And suppose he already married? Danielle said no. He not married because he has not met her yet. This is the man God sent me.

Mr. Nick stood up and he looked out of the window. "Do you know who that young man is?" No. She told him she do not know him, she had a dream about him a long time ago, and she told her sister Dee and Mom about him and she was coming to New Jersey to find him and get married. Danielle felt that this man is going to be her husband and she felt it deep down into her soul and bones, Danielle sister was worried about the two girls in his arms, she told her that was great at lease someone else want him and she like a challenge.

Mr. Nick "asked did He hear her right."? Yeah. Well do you know who that young man is? Danielle asked so what do that suppose to mean? Mr. Nick you see he is one of the best young man in this area.

Just how did you come all the way to New Jersey and pick him out of all of the other boys? Mr. Nick just let her share something with you. You see Mr. Nick a long time ago when she was about fifteen years old she had a dream about this young handsome man in her dream and it was very vivid just like it was just yesterday. Mr. Nick asked how are you planning on meeting this man.? You see Mr. Nick, he will come to me and Danielle felt that it in the words and God will take care of that. She felt she must stay alert, stand still in her faith, be courageous and be strong.

So Mr. Nick you see faith in God is all you need. And the rest will take care of it self. You know Mr. Nick her Mother told her she was born with a veil over her face and she can see and feel certain thing that no one else can feel. But, she felt that she was born brave because God knew what she had to go through that most folk will never face the same hardships. Danielle, was not worried because God has whispers to her; "Be courage, because he is with her."

Today was a knockout with the thinnest summer haze. Danielle rushed home and took a shower, slipped into; a light-blue short-set combed her hair and put it in a pony-tail. Flipped it over her shoulder, and she ran down stairs and out the door for her jogging which she took each day just to unwind.

When she arrived back home she was feeling very happy and relaxed she felt grateful. She understand that positive and negative feeling come and goes and that okay, it's the way life is. Danielle accepts the good alone with the bad. So, when she feeling depressed, angry, or stress out, she, related to these feelings with an openness and wisdom. She accepts the good alone with the bad. She the first to say never fight the feeling, this too will pass and tomorrow is a new day.

Danielle decided to iron her works clothes for the next day in the kitchen, when she spotted this young man washing her land -law car.

Well her heart started to pound away and she got this adrenal rush. She knew that it was only a matter of time before this Young man would be coming through the door to meet her for the very first time. Danielle, patting her hair Oh! she hope it alright, but it too late now to worry about that after all it is neatness comb and up in a tail.

She waited patiently for God's timing. Danielle felt gladness is a key to God's presence. She felt the joy of Jesus is her strength in the presence is fullness of joy. All of a sudden Napoleon knocked on the door, well her heart skipped a beat and she took her sweet time to go and answer the door. She did not want him to know she was waiting for him to come in. As she open the door she smiled, swallowed, and reached for his hand, "Hi my name is Danielle" He said my name is Napoleon, shaking her hand pressing her fingers tight. She asked him what can she do for him? Napoleon said just a glass of water please, Danielle asked him hot or cold? Napoleon said Just form the fountain.

Danielle passed him the water sliding her fingers down the glass. He looked at Danielle twist his mouth to one side took it and drinks it down and said thank you and walked away. Danielle was expecting him to talk to her. But what can you say to someone you never seem? Danielle felt like she had know him all of her life, But, at lease this was a start in the right directions. She was somewhat disappointed in his attitude, at first site, but no one win them all. What the hack they did not build Rome in just one day so she felt there is no reason to complaint. She felt that he was just checking her out. So now he sees what she looked like. She had a feeling that he will be calling her very soon. Danielle felt she will not chase after him.

The phone ringed three days later and it was an astonishing sound she knew it was him before she picked up the phone. She was all excited when she answered phone. "Hello" Napoleon "I would like to come over and talk to you"? Danielle, Oh she sorrow she was just on her way out of the door, Danielle, can she have a ring check? Napoleon "Yes you May". Danielle kissed the phone and hung it up, and she was smiling all down to the button of her feet. But all the same time her heart was saying please come over, she did not want him to think she was easy;she was trying to play hard to get. She knew that was her reason for come to Jersey anyway. On the other hand he did not know that and that will be her secret for many years to come until she make sure he really liked and loved her the way she like and loved him.

THE DARKEST DAY

*T*he curtains in her hospital room were all open. Danielle had opened them. She looked at the clock again and then got up to see if it was working. Time seemed to stand still. She needed to talk to her husband. She reached across the bed and got the phone. Moments later, he answered it. He immediately asked if she was all right. She told him that everything was fine, but that she was a little lonely. He said he would be back soon; he had just walked over to a friend's house. "Hon, you okay?" he asked.

"Yes, I'm fine," she said. But, what she really wanted to say was, "Please come back." Her apprehensions were growing.

*****

It was a lovely day and they had a good trip, but she was dreading taking that long drive back to Jersey.

April 16, 1995.

She had always felt that her husband and children were her main concern. She had promised herself that when she married and began her own family, they would be her prime interest and her biggest concern. She had made a promise to her husband "to love and cherish him in sickness and in health until death do them part," and that their children would be able to count on them together forever. And now, surprisingly enough, it was much easier not to remember to be caught up in the eye of an accident. The eye of the accident is that one specific area in the center of a twister. All the traffic was moving very peacefully and calmly. Everything around the center is violent and turbulent, however the center remains peaceful. How sweet it would be if we could be calm and serene in the midst of chaos in the eye of the accident. What is the intention and practice? You can tell yourself that you are going to use the experience as an opportunity to remain calm. Danielle felt she had to tell herself that she had to stay strong, but the pain became so unbearable, her body tried to

17

protect her by disassociating from her with the eye of the accident. She had made a commitment to her son to help him buy a house.

*****

On Danielle's seventeenth birthday, she moved away from home for a better life in New Jersey. She landed a job in a hospital and she sent money back to her mother to help support her young sister and brothers. As she spent every day working at a nearby hospital, she began to feel like a workaholic, watching the neighborhood girls her age walking up and down the streets, all decked out in "Minnie-skirts" and "hot pants."

In September of 1981, she started nurses' school and traveled forty miles each way three days a week. There were times when she only had one dollar in her pocket to her name and that was for my tolls. When her son was ten years old, he came to her and said, "Mom, I want to show you how to change a tire on your car, because one day you might have a flat tire on the road to school and you will be able to change it yourself. She looked at him and asked, "How did you learn to change tires? "Daddy showed me the other day and now I want to show you," he said.

"Thank you, sweetie, but my tires are good," Danielle said. "But if you want to show me, why not?"

Her son began to explain everything about how to change a tire and how to tighten the bolts after putting it back on. Afterwards, he told her to change her tire and she did. He looked at her and said, "Mom, now I won't have to worry about you. If you get a flat tire, you will know how to change it." Danielle looked at her young son, gave him a big hug and kissed him on his forehead. "Thank you, son, for worrying about me."

The very next day, Danielle packed the kids off to school, and left for her classes, as her normal routine was traveling down that busy parkway north, forty miles from her house. Suddenly, though, she heard this noise coming from the back of her car and it was hard to control the car. She pulled over on the side of the road, got out of her car and she could not believe her eyes. She had a flat tire! She changed the flat and made it to school in time for her class. She looked up and said, "Thank you, Father, for my son."

*****

Danielle felt she had to work hard for everything. She worked as a nurse's aide on Fridays and Saturdays sixteen hours a day, besides going to college four days a week. One day, she arrived at her day shift and she began to feel very ill and nauseated when she stood up. She decided that if she went to have a diet Pepsi to give her some caffeine, she would feel better, and she came back and continued to care for her patients. She still felt very lightheaded when she stood up to walk, as though she was taking large giant steps, walking on air. Finally, she made it through the first shift, and as she walked over to the next floor to do her second shift, she met one of her doctor friends. He looked at her and asked her what the matter?

"You don't look like yourself. Are you sick?" he asked her. "Yes," she told him. "I feel like a big, tall giant walking on air. Dr. Darius took her blood pressure sitting down and it was 120/90mm. Then he asked her to stand up and he took her blood pressure. It was 80/40. Danielle made it back to the soda machine for some more Pepsi. She knew she needed to take some fluids to bring her blood pressure up as Dr. Darius told her she was overworked and dehydrated and needed to take in as much fluids as she possibly could. He assured her he would take care of her after he saw a few patients on the next floor. Danielle knew he had a history for being very slow, and that by the time he came back to care for her, she could be at home. Danielle told the nurse supervisor that she was sick and unable to work her next shift. The nurse supervisor, Denise Skinner told her to go home and rest and hopes she feels better soon.

Danielle slowly walked to the elevator. She got on the elevator, praying every step of the way, went down to the first floor and walked outside. The fresh air hit her face and she felt better. She thanked God and said, "Please, God, let me make it home all right and please take care of me. Mom told me that God takes care of babies and fools. You know, Father God, I am a fool. With your help, I know I can make it home." Danielle knew she would be able to drive home. But, as she traveled down the road about ten miles from her house, she began to feel like she was going to pass out. She stopped her car and walked around for a few minutes, and she felt better, so she proceeded to travel south down the road toward home. Finally, home at last, she dragged her sick, weak body out of her car, walked up six flights of stairs and sat down on the steps to rest. She felt better, but when she stood up, she felt faint and when she sat down, she felt all right. She began crying as she crawled up the stairs on her knees and into her bedroom. She took off her clothes while sitting on the floor alongside of the bed and crawled in bed beside her husband who was fast asleep from working the night shift the night before and she, too, fell asleep.

Around 2:00 A.m., Danielle had to go to the bathroom. She stood up as she normally did and she began to pass out. She sat down on the floor and started to cry. Her husband jumped up out of his sleep, looking at her as if he thought she was crazy sitting on the floor crying for help.

"Napoleon, please help me. I think I am dying. I have no blood pressure when I stand up." Napoleon put his clothes on and told her he was taking her to the hospital. Then he put her clothes on, carried her down the stairs to the car, and rushed her back to the hospital where she had worked earlier that day.

They arrived in the emergency room at 2:30am and all her co-workers laughed, telling her that she'd had too much to drink. Danielle started to cry and told them she wished she were drunk; then she would just sleep it off. But, that was not the case. She told them that she was very sick and that when she stood up, she had no blood pressure. They all got that sad look on their faces and said, "Don't worry. We will take care of you." They began to run every test on her and they all came back negative, so they decided that she was possibly allergic to her blood pressure medication, as the doctor had been trying her on a new one. They gave her .9ns 1000cc bag and kept her in the emergency room for six hours. Danielle begged them to send her back home and she promised the doctor that if things changed, she would come back and would go see her doctor on Monday morning for follow-up care, and she did. Danielle had to miss valuable time from college and work because everything was blurred and she couldn't even read , and she was seeing double. As time passed, she became stronger, was able to return to her busy schedule, and went on to complete her education. Her first desire was to help her family; she was determined to become a registered nurse with a degree.

In 1989, she continued her education. In 1991, she obtained her Bachelor of Science in Nursing degree from Seton Hall University.

Danielle and Napoleon had to make sure that their children's college education was taken care of. They were all struggling and suffering together, and they had their own home and two new cars. She was unable to stay home and go to college. She felt blessed to have her family support, cheering her on. When she would feel depression creeping up on her, she would call her brother John to make her laugh, and she remembered that one time, he sent her an article about a 91-year-old man who graduated from college with a Bachelor's degree, and that gave her the drive to keep her fire burning a little while longer.

She knew that something was still missing in her life, though. Danielle still prayed, but her relationship with Jesus seemed distant and filled with fear. She knew that God had answered her prayers from time to time, and she had met her dream man. She had prayed for someone loving, and patience. And she had wanted a man to father her children. Danielle felt that God had literally led her to the man in her dream. She believed that Jesus was real and loved his children.

God sees no color, nor rich, or poor. Despite all the sickness, heartaches, and pain, death can be redemptive in that it can force us to search the very depths of our being, where we find Jesus dwelling. However, through sickness, or in sickness, we necessarily find redemption as if sickness were redemption; as if sickness was essential and our spirit would grow. While it is true that we might find God, this is what Danielle has seen and experienced. Most folks are more likely to become embittered, and turn away from Jesus than to view sickness as a spiritual opportunity. Danielle discussed the matter with Napoleon and suggested that they begin attending church again. She was less than enthusiastic, mostly because of earlier experiences, which had disillusioned her about religion. He respected her position, but still found a way to bring a stronger sense of religious belief into their family. They attended a couple of local churches, and became members.

After the kids grew up and went to college, they did not feel satisfied there anymore and they went astray; Danielle's belief about religion would remain, she felt, uncertain for many years.

*****

The man came out from behind her. He was driving a heavy black truck on I 95 North. He hit her car and interrupted her thoughts. He hit her car so hard and knocked it into a concrete guard wall. Her fear of accidents went back a long way. Danielle experienced the floating, the light shining in her face. The bright light blinded her. Her body seemed to be sucking directly inside the light. She had no control over it. She could hear Napoleon yelling out her name and telling her to hang in there: "Hang in there and don't let go!" he yelled at the top of his voice. "I here you calling, Napoleon," she said, but she did not want to go back down there. She yelled back, "Napoleon, up here." *Funny,* she thought, *he does not hear me at all,* and yet she could see and hear him.

She saw blood all over his face. What had happened to his face? She could hear all of them down there, gathered around that body. It looked like her. She could see them down there. They thought she was still down there lying on that stretcher-bed with her broken ribs, and God knew what else. They did not even see her heart jump out of her chest, and she took off and landed. Only God knew where she was at now, some far-out place.

What is the problem? Is there anything wrong with me? she wondered. She had left that banged-up body behind. It was kind of funny to run away and not have anyone stop her, she thought. Danielle felt herself drifting up, very gently – up off the stretcher toward the sky, as light as a balloon. There was a bright light that looked like a thousand little Christmas lights and she was just where she wanted to be. She could see there were folks beyond the lights, but she couldn't see their faces. She could feel that they were happy and very caring folks, and they were waiting for her to come and join them. She just wanted to hang out there; it was so peaceful. They thought that she "walked through the valley of the shadow of death. She feared no evil," and she had no pain. Suddenly, she knew what was holding her back. It was Napoleon.

22

That look on his face was so terrible, and there was blood all over his face, dripping all over his Hawaiian white T-shirt. The grief; she had seen it only once before – the day his older sister crossed over, when he was so hurt, and the tears were streaming down his face.

She wondered as she looked down on him and their children, *Oh, how can I do this to him and the children? How can I allow myself to float on into these beautiful lights, knowing how my family will be destroyed? I wish there was a way I could tell him about the lights and the nice folks and this peaceful place, and maybe he would understand.*

Then he would take that long face off. And he would be happy for her instead of being sad. "Napoleon, I love you," she heard herself say. "But, I'll be happier where I'm going. I'll be safe. You are crying for me. I can't believe you are crying for me." He was calling her name; she could hear him telling her to hang in there.

Danielle looked up into the light and told those nice folks, "Not now, but someday –I promise," she said, still hanging out above that body. "I hear you, Napoleon." She felt like her heart had jumped out of her chest, and she was in pain when she breathed. Oh the pain; the light was brighter, but now Danielle didn't see it. Nevertheless, her heart was beating inside her chest. Danielle just wanted to go back where there was no pain. "Napoleon, what is happening to me? Did you know that my heart jumped out of my chest?"

"No," he said, "you just lost consciousness for a few minutes. And your heart never jumped out of your chest. Hang in there. You will be all right. They are taking you to the hospital first and I will be there later. Just hold on and do not let go!"

They transferred Danielle from the car on a stretcher and into the ambulance. She was transported to the community medical center. She was left again with her thoughts. In the utter loneliness of the day, her thoughts now turned to the accident that had just happened. Would everything be all right? She had heard different stories of folks dying from internal bleeding a few hours after an accident, and they looked perfect on the outside. Shortly afterward, they died.

She thought about other folks like herself and that it could happen to her, too.

23

Nurse's Wings

Danielle guessed what was happening to her. Images of graveyards filled her mind. She conjured up a scene of a headstone with her birthday, and the date she died engraved on it. She could see her self-dressed in her white nurses' uniform with her college pin on it, lying in her coffin. She began wondering about the last rites, something she had done many times before for her patients; now someone would be doing it for her. She tried to figure out why the dying needed to have last rites? Was it to show Jesus they were saved? On the other hand, were they sinners who needed protection from the man with the pitchfork and red fire to burn in hell?

The pain became more severe and death was still nagging at her. She arrived in the emergency room and the nurses and doctors all started to work on her. Danielle remembered begging them to please give her something for the pain, and she felt her body getting weaker and weaker and she was unable to breathe. One of the nurses was trying to take off her gold chains on her arms and around her neck. As they were removing her wedding rings, she said "Please save my rings for me." Danielle felt like she had about 50 -100 pounds of gold on her body, and she was saying to herself, "Why did I have all that junk on me? By the time they get it off, I will be dead." Danielle told the nurses she was going to die. "I'm dying," she said, and she began floating and rising. The nurse came and put a mask over her face. She heard the doctor yelling that all of her veins had collapsed and that they had no way to give her the fluids she needed. "We are going to loose her," he said. Danielle could see her body lying on the stretcher with a mask over her face and the doctors and nurses standing all around the table. One of the doctors was saying that they were losing her; she was in shock. "We need a way to give her some intravenous fluids or she is going to die." A nurse yelled that all of Danielle's veins had collapsed and she could not get an intravenous line into her. The doctor was shouting, " I need to insert a central line." He said he felt a pulse in the right groin, but it was very faint. She was floating off the stretcher, hanging out in the air. The nurses were all racing around the stretcher as if they had on roller skates. They looked as though they'd just seen a ghost. What was all the

24

confusion anyway? Only God knew. *I am a nurse,* Danielle thought. *I know how to insert a line. I have a very good vein over here. Why won't anyone listen to me? I have a vein over here, doctor.* They all could not be brain dead or hard of hearing. Danielle asked herself what was wrong with this picture anyway. *I feel sorry for that poor person on that stretcher,* she thought. *And that big needle would kill me. That has to be very painful to her and I am so glad it is she and not I being stuck.*

Danielle remembered that she heard one of the nurses yelling, "Come back! Wake up! You are all right now and we are giving you some fluids and we are going to take you for a Cat-scan now."

They were wheeling her down a long cold hallway and she felt every movement on the floor. Shortly after she arrived in this large white room, they slid her off the stretcher on to a hard, cold table. They all left the room. Danielle could feel the table being engulfed by this big white, cold, and hard machine.

The next thing she knew, they were taking her back to her room. One of the nurses told her that the doctor was going to put a tube in her chest because one of her lungs had a hole in it. She started crying and asked them please not to do it now. The nurse told her she was going to leave the chest tube at Danielle's bedside for the time being, but if she started to have a problem breathing, they would have to insert it in her chest. Danielle said all right. She asked for pain medication and was afraid to complain about having a problem breathing. She would just lay there taking baby breaths while holding her lungs close to her side, and every time the nurse would take her pulse and oxygen level, she prayed for them to be all right.

Finally, they brought her husband into the emergency room and put him on the other side of the curtain. Danielle heard her husband asking the nurse how is my wife doing? She told him that she would push the curtain back and he could see for himself. He had told her to fight to stay alive, telling her she could do it. Danielle told him she was all right. (As she found out much later, Napoleon's head and face got cut from the shattering of the windshield and he had glass all over his body. He had scars all over his head and face that lasted for a very long time. He told her that when he would go out, people would be staring at him. But, he was glad to be alive. He had no broken bones, but he looked very sick.) As for Danielle, she didn't have a scar on her body, but she had a lot of broken bones and black and blue marks. Their lives were change forever – within a blink of an eye.

But right now, she was drifting in and out and was very drowsy. Finally, she was able to speak with Napoleon and tell him she was okay. Napoleon told her he was praying for her. She told him she was praying for him and herself to survive.

Danielle wanted to feel the pain from time to time; that would mean that she was still alive. She had to hold her left side to support her rib area so that she would be able to breathe, and she was unable to move on her own.

The Next Day

$\mathcal{M}$orning came quickly, with the doctors all dressed in white coats, making their rounds. For a moment, Danielle thought she was home, but then realized that she was in another hospital and a long way from home.

The nurses transferred Danielle to the critical care trauma unit and put her on a morphine PCA pump. She slept most of the day and night and was still drowsy from all those heavy-duty drugs. Or perhaps she felt exhausted from all the X-rays, Cat-scans, and fear and anxiety from the day before. But, the following day, she was taken to her own room, and she relaxed and began to reflect on the last time she had been in the hospital. Her fear of the recent darkness had been slight compared to her fear back then. At least this time, she knew what was supposed to happen.

Napoleon was discharged from the hospital and their son took him back to Jersey for a few days to recuperate, while she struggled to get better each day. Danielle felt the need to get off the morphine drip; she wasn't able to think clearly and she felt the need to sleep a lot, and she had wild dreams. Four days later, after she was in and out of the comatose-like state from the morphine drip, Danielle finally got enough strength to put on her nurse's call light and she asked the nurse to please call the pain management department and ask for some other kind of pain medication.

The pain management team brought in this small device called a T.E.N.'s unit which sends out electric shock waves to the brain and helps your body get rid of some of the pain by stimulating blood to the area. The nurse put an ice pack on top of the device.

Twenty-six hours later, Danielle began to experience hallucinations: Bugs were crawling on the walls and drapes by her bedside. Danielle put her nurse's call light on and was yelling at the top of her voice. A nurse came running into her room to see what was the matter. She told the nurse about the bugs and that she was feeling nauseated. It took the nurse an hour to calm her down. She reassured Danielle that there were no bugs in her room – that it was just from the medications she had taken. Danielle felt better after talking with the nurse, who reminded Danielle that she was experiencing a reaction from the Percocet. The registered nurse left her light on in her room.

Danielle began to feel stronger and more awake during the day, and her doctor started her on a full liquid diet. She was trying to remember the last time she had spoken to her sisters or brothers. Her twin brothers had visited with her the day of the accident and a few days later, and she put on her nurse's call light to see if there was a problem with her phone. Now that Danielle was feeling better, she started to worry about her family back home. She had not heard from them in a few days. She returned back to the nurses' station to check her phone. Shortly after she came back to her room, the operator told her that her family had asked her to hold all calls. They wanted her to rest for a few days. Danielle thought that made sense.

Danielle was discharged from the hospital after 12 days and she began looking for a doctor who would accept her, and he ordered nurses, a nurse's assistant and a physical therapist to come into her home for the next two weeks. She worked very hard to get her body back into shape. Danielle felt pain in every bone in her body. Her left ribs were broken, her left shoulder rotation cuff was torn, the left side of her nose was torn and stiff, and she had strains and sprains, and a contusion from head to toes.

Twelve days later, Danielle was strong enough to be transported back home. She worked hard to gain her strength back at the rehabilitation facility. Danielle felt helpless having people drive her around and her nurse's assistant walking in her shadow. Her family gave her a new name: Mrs. B. Danielle. The family was there to cheer her on. It was good to be back home and sleep in her own bed. She was grateful to feel the pain; that way, she knew she was alive.

Hold On To Faith

ays went by and Danielle was moving rather slowly. She had encouraged her son to give up his place and they would help him buy a house, and he could rent out some of it to have extra money for school. But, now she was unable to work and she didn't have the money for the closing. Her husband came to her. She could see the hurt in his eyes and hear the hurt in his voice. It was painful for him to tell her this. She asked what was the matter? "Are you okay?"

He said, "No, we have a problem and I do not know how to say this without upsetting you. It's time that you face reality and wake up from this dream you're living in."

She began to panic. She said to her self, "Does he know something about my body or what happened to me that I don't know?" "What are you trying to tell me?" she asked him. "Are you trying to tell me you are walking out on me?"

"Of course not. I will never leave you."

Napoleon then told her that things were not getting better financially and they would be unable to help buy the house for Jr. He could not see where the money was coming from for the closing with her being unable to work now, and unable to take the long drive.

"Okay, Napoleon, you made your point," she said.

"I want you to get the money back and forget about buying the house," said Napoleon.

"No, you see I promised JR. that I was going to help him buy a house and I will not go back on my word," said Danielle. "I will find a way. I'll get a loan."

Napoleon asked, "How are you going to get a loan, with no job?" "I will find a way, Napoleon. Just wait and see."

Napoleon said, "You almost died trying to buy that house. You just do not get it! Is there a message trying to tell you something?" "Yes," said Danielle. "The message tells me that I will do it or die, and only Jesus can stop me by ripping my tongue out of my mouth, or death." Danielle felt this was just a test from Jesus trying to make her stronger, and testing her faith in him. She might not be able to work as a nurse right now, but she would find a way. There is *always* a way.

Danielle had just finished eating dinner, and she became all choked up as if her food had backed up in her throat. She did not want Napoleon to know that he had really hurt her. It was like he had stabbed her and left her to die. She fought back her tears and immediately asked him to help her back to her room.

She just sat very quietly and prayed for Jesus to please, please help her. As she prayed, she said, "Father God, I need you to come into my life and into my heart. Please make my faith, soul, body and mind strong in your name, of Jesus." Danielle felt she needed help, and only God could give it to her. The tears rolled down her cheeks and she was choking on her secretions as she tried to hold back the tears. She asked God to lead her to the answer.

She reached into her bookstand for something to read, and the first thing she picked up was: "*Try Faith and Watch What Happens.*" It was an inspirational booklet no more than eighty pages. She read it from front to back, and the more she read it, the more it sounded just like her and Napoleon's problem. When she finally finished reading it, she asked Napoleon if he would bring the boxes from the filing cabinet downstairs, and put them on the kitchen table for her in the morning before he went to work.

Napoleon said, "Why, sure. Is there anything else you want me to do?" "No," she replied. Danielle prayed for her family and she thanked Jesus for sparing her life. She felt that God had left her on earth for a reason, and the only thing that came to her mind was that she had to finish her mission – the job she had started on, buying a house for her son.

The next morning she arouse early, and asked her husband to help her into the kitchen so she could check out the boxes. She started to open old letters – junk mail – throwing it out. Suddenly, she had a strong feeling that she had misplaced something useful.

Finally, she came across this letter from a life insurance company, telling her that the company was going out of business and they were returning her money. And this was the second letter. She called up the company and the person who answered the phone told her the company has closed and they gave her another number to call and they told her the woman who handled that matter was on vacation for two weeks.

Danielle had been out of work for two months and she had not seen the first disability check; her funds were running low. She could not understand what was going on with her husband. Although she refused to accept it, tears started rolling down her cheeks. She was thanking Jesus for what he had done for her and not letting her husband discourage her about buying the house.

Danielle ran to the phone and called her husband. "Are you sitting down?" she asked.

He said "No."

"Well, sit down," she said. She received a blessing from Jesus, and she told him the good news. Napoleon asked her not to read too much into that letter and to calm down, and wait until she got the check in her hands.

She put in another call to the new company and they told her that the person who handled the funds was also on vacation for two weeks. Danielle were asked to call back in two weeks.

In the meantime, she continued to believe that things were going to work out in her favor, so for the next ten days, Danielle read the small book *Try Faith and Watch What Happens.*

She remembered that one of her patients once told her a story about an old man and his sister who lived together in this big, beautiful white house, and one day, her brother had a stroke, and found it hard to communicate with his sister. But from time to time, he would say, "Look up, look up." They were very poor and had spent most of their funds, and she was struggling just to care for him and keep a roof over their heads.

Nevertheless, one day he died and his sister had no money, and no food. And the city was trying to take her home away. The woman fell to her knees and began to pray, and afterwards, she was able to struggle back to her feet. The old woman remembered her brother dying words. He was telling her to look up. She struggled up into the attic, her body stricken with arthritic pain. Her hands shook as she looked into this old dusty, dirty box. There was her brother's old black Bible. She wiped the dust away, and on the very first page was one thousand dollars. She continued to turn the pages and on every page was one thousand dollars, and she started thanking God and crying.

There will come a time when you will have to follow your own dream and have faith in Jesus.

Napoleon and her children were great about helping her around the house. She knew she had to help herself, and every chance she could get, she was working out in the rehabilitation center.

They bought the house and had enough money to buy a new Whirlpool washer and dryer, a refrigerator, and new carpet throughout this ten room bi-level house.

On August 18, 1995, Danielle was able to go back to work fulltime, in her position as a registered nurse. She knew that she had to return to the hospital to have surgery on her left shoulder and left knee. But, she was so glad Jesus had given her a second life and she was so glad to be alive. Danielle took one day at a time and embraced the moment, just enjoying the fresh air and being able to breathe without pain. She felt that was a great blessing for her.

Danielle felt that she had gone through the storms in her life with little hope for the future, and she sometimes wondered if her life would ever be the same again, Storms and family problems, times of spiritual lows, long periods of family illness and dying, and accidents, all can cause one to feel hopeless, and that there is no reason to go on. But there is that small voice on the inside telling you that everything will be all right – just have faith in God. He will take care of you; just hold on.

Danielle felt at times that she could not withstand the rain falling on her windowpane. But, she remembered as a little child being told that "This, too, shall pass" and God would send sunshine again and it would be better than it was before. Just hold on, hold on – you'll see.

Bless These Hands

*T*he following year, on May 4, 1996, Danielle returned to the hospital to have the surgery on her shoulder and knee. She was frightened and nervous. Napoleon had taken the day off from his job and stayed right by her bedside. She asked him to please pray with her and for her. On the afternoon of the surgery, a nurse came in and prepared her for surgery and gave her a shot to put her to sleep. Then she transferred her to the operating room. Danielle could hear the doctors and nurses talking and the medication traveling through her veins. Finally, she fell into a deep sleep.

When she awakened, the doctor was at her bedside telling her that the surgery was over and that he had started her on a morphine pump for pain, and she should be feeling fine in a few days and be able to go home.

Danielle said, "This is the best news I have heard today. This is a blessing." Now, she could finally try to rest, and stop thinking about the pain, and she drifted off to sleep.

That night, she awakened and looked around. She was in a private room at the end of the hallway called the north end. The room was peacefully decorated, with bright blues, pale blues, dark blues and off-white wallpaper – relaxing and peaceful. Danielle noticed one nightstand, one closet, a television set with a video-player, and large windows on the sides of her room. She had asked for a private room with a lot of windows because ever since her car accident, she had suffered from claustrophobia. It was dark outside, and the only light shining in her room was the moonlight on the side of her bed. Danielle rang for the nurse and asked her to open the drapes in front of her bed. She had closed the drapes earlier so she could fall asleep, but she had no recollection of sleeping. The nurse said that Danielle's family and friends had been visiting with her and left twelve long-stemmed roses along with carnations, and a beautiful green plant. But Danielle could not remember seeing any visitors. Her hair was a mess and her hospital gown barely covered her. She really did not appreciate people seeing her when she was not aware they were there. She talked to her sister and husband and asked them not to bring her friends around at a time like this.

At 6:00 in the morning, the nurse brought her medications in, all except pain pills, and disconnected the morphine PCA pump. She checked her surgical sites for bleeding, and they were okay. Danielle took the pills and settled down to get a little snooze before her busy day started. She must have dozed off because when she looked at her watch, it was eight thirty. She put her nurse's call light on and asked the nurse to come and help her with her daily living activities. She was excited about going home. Danielle put in a call to Napoleon and asked him to come and pick her up. She didn't even eat her breakfast; she just wanted to go home. She felt like taking a walk down the hallway to the nursing station to wait for Napoleon to arrive.

"You're finally here," she said when Napoleon came. "And I am ready to go home."

Their son, JR., came down from Buffalo, New York, to help care for her for a few days, until she got stronger. She felt that this was a piece of cheesecake. She had her son there with her and they could catch up on old times. And he could take her to the hairdresser, and from there, they would go shopping for a few items she needed around the house. She felt like a super mom. It was her doctor's orders to do a lot of walking and not just lay around in bed taking pain pills, falling asleep, and most of all, feeling sorry for herself.

Danielle felt she could vacuum her house, using the machine as her crutch, and put it on automatic and let it go. She saw nothing wrong with that. So what if she could only use her right side? She felt that she would make the best of what she had.

The eight days ended so fast and JR. left for college. His sister, Melissa, called for her two weeks of duty. She said, "Mom, I have my bags all packed and ready to leave now." Danielle talked her out of coming home. She told Melissa that her brother had just left, and that she would be fine; there was no need for her to come. She could get around without her, and finally, Melissa agreed.

Danielle said to herself, "Why are they so worried about me? I am not worried about myself, and after all, I am a nurse and can really take care of myself. What I do best is care for folks who are sick in the hospital." Danielle felt she knew she could take care of herself, even though she only had her right side in good working condition, so what was all the to-do about anyway?

Dark, Cold Crushing Walls

Saturday, May 18, 6 a.m.

Suddenly, a little light tapping at the foot of her bed awakened Danielle. She just lay in her bed thinking to herself, "What does my dog want now? It is to early for him to go outside." She felt that if she lay still, he would let her get another snooze, and come back later to wake her up. But, a few seconds later, she felt this tickling on the bottom of her feet. She remembered when she was a child, she had experienced the tickling on the bottom of her feet and she would peep from under the covers and see her grandmamma at the foot of her bed, dressed all in white with those small wire frame glasses. All right, what is going on? She wondered as she began to sit up.

Danielle felt this thing jump on her legs. She tried to move, and reach for the phone and yelling, but the words would not come out. And this fuzzy thing was moving up on her body and began kissing her all over her face. Danielle felt so cold, and dirty; she felt this heavy object pressing on her chest. It felt like the Empire State building had taken up residence right in the center of her chest and it was pushing all the air out of her lungs. She started to blame herself for promising her daughter she could care for herself, and now this. Danielle knew she had to hang on and she felt impending doom. She just hoped her daughter would forgive her if she died without saying goodbye. She thought about her son and her poor husband coming home and finding her dead. However, Danielle said to herself, no one lived forever and if it was time for her to go, she had to go.

She was fully awake and alert. She tried to move from under the heavy weight, but was unable to. She tried to open her eyes but was unable to. Danielle tried yelling at the top of her voice, but the words just would not come out.

She thought about what her mother had told her one-day before she died: she told Danielle about how one night, she could not catch her breath and she was in a lot of pain, and there was this place with a lot of bright sparkling lights shining all around her. She said she did not panic, and she just took little breaths and finally, she could breath again.

Danielle felt the room was very cold and dark. She felt herself becoming lifeless, her body growing limp. She tried to reach the phone near the bed in attempt to call her husband. She was unable to free this heavy thing off her chest. She felt a frightening sensation, like every breath she took would be her last breath, and the pressure continued to press harder and harder and deeper into her weak, hollow chest. She felt hopeless and lifeless, and most of all, she was frightened because she was home alone.

Then she felt her body crushed together like sardines in a can in this cave. It was very dark in there she felt the cold concert closing in all around her body and she was in a tight, narrow tunnel. Danielle's first impression was that she was still alive because she could feel the pain. But, she still felt the weight of the Empire State Building sitting in the center of her chest and she was unable to move. She got this adrenal rush, and her brain started to download like a computer and she didn't even have to click on the mouse. She started to remember when she was a little girl all dressed up in her pink coat and bonnet, and shiny baby-doll black leather shoes.

Danielle started to remember the first little black Bible she had as a young child, in the third grade. She thought to herself that this was the real thing, and she felt she was being buried alive, like a cavewoman, and no one would hear her cry. She said to herself, "Okay, this is the real thing and I am dying slowly by degrees." As she was lying paralyzed from head to toe, she thought about the old song her mom used to sing in church about Jesus knowing all about our struggles. Yes!! Big Brother knew all about her. She did not have to open her mouth. He knew what she was thinking about before the words came out of her mouth. She felt it was time for her to leap out on faith.

The Silent Prayer

anielle felt she had a spiritual connection with God, and as she began to silently pray, she heard rushing noises around her bed, like the sound of the ocean tides. There were wings flopping from the top of her bed, on her left side to the bottom of her feet. As she lay there listening to the noises, she prayed for God to give her life back. She felt that God would look after her. She put her faith in Him and she started to pour her heart out.

She knew a man and his name was Jesus. "Father God, help me believe that there is no situation so hopeless that it cannot be transformed by your power." She continued to pray.

She thanked Jesus for sharing his big beautiful world with her. She thanked him for everything she had and the things she did not have, and her lovely family -- her mother and father, even though they both had gone on to be with God. She thanked Jesus for her husband and her two lovely children, and her brothers and sisters. She thanked him for bringing her into his world.

Danielle thought back about her little black Bible which said that the Lord giveth and the Lord taketh away. "Blessed be the name of the Lord. I thank you for sending the Angels to watch over me. If I have hurt or said anything to hurt anyone, please forgive me. Jesus, please do not let me be having a stroke. Jesus, if it is your will, please let it be done." Oh, she could not take the pain. "If I am going to die, please take me right now. Who am I? I am no better than my father, my mother, my sister and my four brothers. I put my life in your hands. Take me and do whatsoever you will. I'm your child and you are my Father in heaven."

She gave up and lay there waiting for a change to come. She felt that she did not want anyone to pity her, nor did she want to be a burden to her family. Danielle felt the tunnel get darker and darker, and very much tighter. But suddenly, she felt a calm feeling come over her.

She said, "Okay, this is it." Danielle felt she should just lie back and enjoy the ride and she felt a blast of cold air out of this cold cave. She felt different from her past near-death experience. She felt no pain, but so different. This cold, dark tunnel was darker. It wasn't the lack of light; it was a dense blackness unlike her consciousness told her that she should be terrified; that all of the fear of her youth should have risen up. With this darkness, she felt intense. And a sense of well-being and calmness.

Danielle felt herself moving forward through it, and the ocean sounds completely disappeared – the popping in the ears like when an airplane takes off, going up into the air. Danielle felt her ears calm down. She was lying on her back with a pillow under her

head, moving very fast, as if she were on a runaway train, head first, the same way she came into the world. She felt as light as a bird feather. She felt peaceful and happy and she felt she would like to hang out there for a while, and know that if she wanted to, she could. But, how could she stay there without her husband and children? She knew that they would be very sad and angry with her, for leaving them without even a goodbye.

Danielle could not begin to understand what was happening to her. She wasn't even sick. She felt no pain and wondered what she was doing there. This was not some crazy dream she was having, was it? This was the real thing. She must be dead, but how could this be? She was not even sick.

THE EYE OF AN ANGEL

*T*he eye of an angel. Danielle saw this unearthly light, from a distance, and she seemed to be drawn into it like a whirlwind. It was a strong and overpowering feeling of love, peace, and well- being. There were brilliant colors, twilight – the green and blue colors. The closer, it got toward her, the light became brighter.

There were fresh fragrances, like nothing she had ever smelled before. The fresh scent of roses, sweet, smelling in the air. It was sweeter than a rose garden. And Sweet smelling like a candy factory.

All of a sudden, out of nowhere, Danielle heard the noise of the flopping of big bird wings. She was very surprised to hear and see all the Angels, and they were dressed in whiter-than-white feather robes.

"Dear Father God in Heaven, when I decided to believe in and trust in you, I thought you would take care of me, and now I'm here all by myself and this is as low as I can get. What do you want me to do?"

Danielle was unable to move any part of her weak body. She had felt that she and God had a relationship of an unconditional love that was real and very special to her. Danielle felt that it was a kind of ideal relationship in which she felt loved. She felt that no matter what she looked like or felt like and sounded like. God was there with her.

"Now, God, you left me here all alone with no one to care for me."

She just didn't get it, nor could she understand any of this. She felt like an abandoned broken-up and no good rag doll. She felt, who would want this broken and cut-up cold shell? She was stuck inside it, unable to escape. But, this was not as bad as she thought, being stuck behind these dark, crunched up walls, and she had never been there before. She would just hang out there and wait for the Angels to take her home. Danielle felt she must have wings, too.

"Who am I anyway?"

Danielle felt the Angels rush to the top, left side and to the foot of her bed. They sounded and looked like a group of birds, dressed in pure white robes made of feathers.

She felt it must be time to get ready because the Angels had brought her some news. She felt a calm, peaceful relieved feeling.

She remembered reading in her little black Bible as a child that Jesus said he would not leave you nor forsake you. As she lay there, unable to move, Danielle felt she would just wait and see what happened next. She felt no pain so she guessed she was dead now, but "This too shall pass." She felt that a change was going to come and she did not fear what lay ahead of her.

The weather was hazy, cloudy, and dusty-dark, with mist in the air. She heard the flopping of the Angels' wings come rushing around her bed. Each took their place from the top of her head to the bottom of her feet. There was this sweet smell in the air. It was like something she had never smelled before. She looked to her left side and she saw the Angels; she looked to her right and saw this very tiny light, smaller than an eye. As it moved closely toward her, the eye became larger and larger, and all of a sudden, the lights were sparkling all around it. She could not take her eyes off it. It became brighter and it was so bright – brighter than the sun and brighter than anything she could ever imagine.

There was a bright twilight, and as the bright light moved near her it became higher and larger, out stepped Jesus all dressed in a pure white robe. No wrinkles, just this perfectly smooth and pinkish-tan color skin and hazy light-brownish color eyes. She had never seen that color brown before on anyone. Danielle would never forget those eyes. A large crowd of people was following him.

Danielle thought about the woman in the Bible who said that if she could touch the hem of Jesus' garment, she would be made whole. Danielle felt a need to touch the hem of his garment. She felt so happy to see him coming. As Jesus walked alone on the right side of her bed, Danielle struggled to move her right arm just to touch his garment. "I touched him. I touched him and now I will be all right." Danielle could feel the tears rolling down her cheeks and now she knew that she was alive and could feel the pain once again. Her thoughts raced on, and she felt so elated.

"Jesus loves me. He will never leave me," she said as tears ran down her cheeks.

Danielle felt the Jesus that she had feared ever since her younger years. He was nothing like she had thought; he was an almighty, good God.

Who am I to question Jesus about the why, and what has happened to me? She thought. Danielle would not say, "Why me?" Nor would she say, "Why not me?" She had banked on faith in God and He arrived on time. Danielle remembered her mother teaching her when she was a little girl that when God was doing His work, you just had to be quiet and wait until He finished his job.

She was raised in the deeply rooted Southern soil of Alabama. As such, she defied even the stereotyped image of a Southern belle. As a child, she could still remember the storms that would come up every day in the hot summer time. The sky would get very dark and black; then all of a sudden, the lightening would light up the entire sky. It was like the Fourth of July fireworks in Jersey.

Danielle felt light as if she could fly. Afterwards, she was able to move off her bed as if someone had lifted her. The weight lifted off her chest. She was able to stand up once again on her feet, using her crutch. She felt the Angels as they let her go. She just felt the tears rolling down her cheeks, and she began to thank God for coming to take care of her when she was home all alone. Danielle had read somewhere in a book that God would never let you be alone. All you had to do was reach out, and He would be right there. Danielle could witness just that.

She felt as light as a feather. But, she felt very weak and had to sit back down on her bed. She could not believe what had happened to her? The pain was gone. It was like nothing she had ever experienced before. She felt Jesus knew when she needed him and he came and took care of her. She took her crutch on the right side of her bed and walked down the hallway into the kitchen. She stood in the kitchen for a few minutes, trying to figure out whom she could call. But how could she tell anyone what had happened to her? They might think she was off her rocker from taking too many drugs. Danielle refused to think about going back to the hospital; she disliked being stuck like a pincushion for blood every six hours.

Danielle felt she would just take a pill and go back to bed. As she started to walk back to her bedroom, she felt a slight pain coming back. She returned back to the medicine cabinet and took one carisprodol 350mg tablet for muscle relaxation and a Tylenol-#3 for pain. Then she walked slowly back down the hallway into her room. She no longer felt afraid of dying. About two hours later, she awakened and felt no pain.

Danielle got up, reached for her crutch and slowly walked down the hallway. She felt like she was walking on ice and was afraid she was going to break any second now.

I Touched Him

anielle saw now that nothing was impossible for God if you had faith and believed. Finally, she awakened and she felt no pain. She was able to sit up and reach her crutch alongside of her bed. She walked down the hallway and into the living room and sat on the sofa waiting for her husband to arrive home from work. She felt this crisis had come out of nowhere. As she sat there, she wondered how she could tell her husband about what had happened to her. She felt he would just think it was the side effects from her pain medication, but she knew deep down in her heart that it was as real as it could be.

She had been following her doctor's orders, walking and exercising, drinking eight glasses of water a day, staying out of bed most of the day, and even doing house work. Her husband arrived from work, and she told him that a strange thing had happened to her. It was like nothing she had ever experienced before. Jesus and his Angels had come to see her. She had gotten very sick and she died.

Her husband was looking at her very oddly.

Danielle was yelling at the top of her voice, and the words just would not come out. "The Angels and Jesus came to see me today and I was able to reach out my right hand and touch his garment as he passed by my bed, like the woman in the Bible."

Her husband's facial expression said it all. Danielle felt he thought the pain medication was playing tricks with her mind. He just listened patiently, with tears in his eyes. He said, "Okay, did you call your doctor and tell him what had happened?"

"No, it is something very serious and I know he will put me back into the hospital," she said, "and I just left the hospital 11 days ago."

Napoleon turned to her and asked, "What do you think happened to you?"

Danielle told him she thought she had a blood clot in her leg, which broke off and traveled to her lungs, and she thought that was why she was unable to breathe, so she died and the Angels and Jesus came. She said that they took care of her. They saved her life and sent her back to him. Tears were rolling down her cheeks and her heart became heavy as she was speaking, and then she became all choked up.

"You know, Napoleon, I am not afraid of dying anymore," she said. However, she promised him that if the pain came back, she would call her doctor and tell him about her symptoms and about Jesus and the Angels, too, and about the feeling of doom.

Danielle felt that as a nurse, she could use her knowledge to help someone in pain and tell him or her not to panic – that they needed to save their oxygen, and if possible, take little breaths instead of large breaths. She wanted to stress most of all that they should keep their wits and not panic, because this just might save their life.

Danielle felt that God had stopped by and told her not to worry or be afraid because He was with her, and He would never leave her; He would make her strong and He would help her when she was down and would pick her up. She wanted people to know that when you are unable to walk, He will carry you. He will be there right beside you holding your hand. Just don't be afraid. You will feel better soon –just you wait and see.

Danielle became a great believer in God and she trusted Him. He never left her alone and most of all, when she called upon Him, He came. She felt that whenever she called on Him in time of need, she could feel His presence – a cool breeze coming or a unique smell, and there were times when He appeared in her dreams or her inner consciousness.

Danielle felt that with everything that had happened to her, Jesus was making her a better person. She felt that Jesus was making her over just like someone would be making a cheesecake. He was putting the best ingredients in a bowl and mixing it up.

Danielle was so confused and mixed up; she had no clue as to what she was really supposed to be doing or where she was heading. She was waiting to see what the end would be.

The Touch of Fate

A t times, Danielle felt as though her life had been nothing but trials and tribulations. Starting with a slight chest pain, sweating, and difficulty breathing. Danielle reached beside her bed for her crutch and hopped over to open her bedroom window to get some fresh air. Then she raced down the hallway, and the chest pain was getting worse and she was having more of a problems breathing.

Danielle yelled, crying for Napoleon. She forgot that she had sent him out to the store. She called her doctor and she was trying to tell him about her past experience. This morning, she felt the pressures coming back and pain crushing all the air out of her lungs. Danielle was unable to catch her breath and she wasn't able to tell her doctor what had happened early that morning. As she was about to collapse on the floor, the door opened and Napoleon walked in just in time. She was unable to speak and her mind was racing around in circles jabbering and crying, "nurse down," as she struggled to stay on her feet. She refused to wait for death. Danielle thought about one of her patients who tried to run from death by leaving the hospital. He had told Danielle that he refused to stay in bed and wait for death. He was going to stay up and walk out of the hospital. He said he never knew anyone who had died walking – they always died lying down.

Napoleon came rushing into the room and picked up the phone and told the doctor what had happened to Danielle. Dr. Skiller asked Napoleon to bring her to the emergency room right away and for her to be prepared to stay in the hospital. He would be calling her orders into the hospital right away.

Danielle knew she had to go back into the hospital and only God knew if she would live or die this time around. After all, how many shots do you get in a lifetime? She felt she had used all of her shots. There was this stabbing, heavy feeling in her chest, as her husband watched her struggling to breathe. Finally, they arrived at the hospital. Napoleon rushed out of the car and grabbed a wheelchair. He helped her get into it and took Danielle inside the emergency room. One of the nurses greeted her and took her back into a room. Danielle was placed on a stretcher. You could hear her breathing all the way down the corridor. Dr. Jonathan came rushing in to check her oxygen and pulse oximetry and found that her oxygen saturation was holding at between 70% and 78% on room air . The nurse placed her on a face mask and it came up to 92%. Her resting heart rate was 130 beats per minute. She had obvious right-side heart failure. She had jugular distention while she was in the high fowler's position. Her respiratory rate was in the 30's to 40's.

How long could she struggle without respiratory or even cardiac arrest? Dr. Blake, the third year resident, was saying that she might have to be intubated and placed on a ventilator. Danielle said, "Please, no tube." Then Dr. Blake ordered that her artery blood gases should be tested. Danielle was praying that the artery blood gases would be at least in the 80's. She did not even feel the needle when Dr. Blake drew her artery blood gases from her wrist and normally, that is very painful.

The nurse, Beth, said, "Slapped a cardiac monitor on her chest." The nurse, Kinda, checked her oxygen level. The resident rushed into the room and the nurse informed him that Danielle's oxygen level was only 80%.

The resident informed her that he needed to draw artery blood gases. The nurse inserted an intravenous line in her other arm. The resident then told the nurse to bolus her with 10,000 units of Heparin and started an intravenous Heparin drip at 15000u/hr. via pump.

The nurse informed the resident that Danielle's pulse oximetry level on arrival was 80% and dropping, before she placed her on a face mask. The doctors were talking about putting her on a life support intubation and mechanical ventilation if her oxygen level continued to drop to a dangerously low level an she become hypoxemia. Danielle knew they would be intubating her, at which time they would put her on a life support mechanical ventilation to keep her alive. She knew that would be her only hope to keep her alive and she could even die in the process.

It made her think about her late father —how he must have felt when he became very ill. He had to be intubated and placed on mechanical ventilation for difficulty breathing and all of a sudden, he had to be placed on a life support machine in order to breathe, too. She remembered her dad telling his doctor that he never wanted to be placed on a life support mechanical again.

Danielle was taken to the chest X-ray department. Someone from the admitting department was chasing behind the stretcher to find out what kind of insurance she had. And it was taking every breath for her to stay alive. Why did those admitting department folks keep following her and asking all those demanding questions? *What is wrong with them?* she thought angrily. "Can't they see I'm having problems breathing and have chest pains?" But they insisted that she sign ten sheets of paper. Hadn't anyone ever told them that if you drop dead, they would not be able to sue you nor send your bill to a collection agency to pay the hospital bills? She never knew anyone yet who had an address in the cemetery. She thought that was off- limits for the mail carrier.

Dr. Blake told her that the chest X-ray showed that something was definitely wrong with her lungs. Napoleon was frantic and asked Danielle what she thought was wrong. "From the X-rays, it looks like I have pneumonia or cancer," she told Napoleon. "But I myself think I have blood clots in my lungs, and they are blocking off my arteries and veins and that is what is making it hard for me to breathe. I could die any minute. My risk factors –car accident, high blood pressure, and shoulder and knee surgery – most likely contributed to lower-extremity venostasis."

Since the accident, Danielle had been very active and spent most of her time out of bed and walking around, going shopping with Jr. and doing the housework with one hand. She said, "Napoleon, I have never had a problem breathing before until I had this surgery and it had to come from a blood clot or phlebitis that came from my legs, broke off and traveled to my lungs. On the other hand, if I have cancer, I would have lost weight, have dyspnea, hoarseness, fatigue, and anorexia."

Danielle had no chills, nor fever and Dr. Skiller tested her lungs through his stethoscope, and heard an accentuated pulmonic second sound, so he suspected a multiple pulmonary embolism. She had presented with shortness of breath and chest pressure upon arrival at the community medical center. She had diaphoresis, tachycardia, tachypneic, and hypoxic, and rhonchi bi-lateral lungs. Her chest-X-ray was positive for pneumonia or cancer, and her electrocardiogram was negative for an acute ischemic event, However, she had continuing hypoxia. As a cardiac critical care nurse, she knew that the results of her V/Q scan would be positive for bloods clots. He gave her 8mgs of morphine intravenously immediately for the pain. The doctor felt that he could continue to treat her with the Heparin drip as ordered before. She told her husband, "Most people don't live to talk about this and most of them are unable to make their own decision. Sometimes I think about how many people have come through those doors and never knew what hit them, and their family members find out weeks later that they had a pulmonary embolism (PE) diagnosed after an autopsy.

The Love of a family

anielle was very close to her older sister and even more, now, since their mother had died, and she knew that her sister would tell her other brothers and sisters that she was sick and back in the hospital. Then Beth, the nurse, transported her to one of the critical care units with the cardiac monitor that sounded like a fire engine, all down the corridor.

When Danielle arrived in the unit, it was like lightning had struck her down flat on her chest and all the air came out of her lungs. The pain was so severe and sudden that each breath brought agony. Danielle felt that the end of her life was near. She wheezed like the old black tea kettle in her mother's kitchen in the deep south of Alabama. Her friend Hope came in to place the cardiac monitor on her, but Danielle was sweating, suffering and struggling to breathe. Hope became frightened and left the room in a hurry.

Her two brothers, Jasha and Jason, arrived and saw her gasping for air, coughing and thrashing around in her bed. She heard Jasha tell Jason and her husband, "We have to pray for her."

Jasha asked Napoleon to place his right hand on her left shoulder Jasha placed his left hand on her right shoulder and they both held Jason's hand.

Danielle remembered her instructions when she went to nursing school about therapeutic touch, and now her brother was using it on her. Jasha began to pray for Jesus to ease her pain and to give her strength to face what lay ahead of her. She felt her life slowly slipping away with every breath she took. She felt so exhausted and helpless from struggling to exhale or inhale. She just wanted to fall asleep. Her brothers and her husband gathered around her bed and them all held hands.

Jasha lead the prayers and Jason and Napoleon repeated after him. Jasha prayed, as he had never heard before.

The Lords Prayer

Our Father which art in heaven, Hallowed be thy name.
Thy Kingdom come, Thy will be done, on earth, as it is in heaven.
Give us this day our daily bread
And forgive us our debts, as we forgive our debtors.
And lead us not into temptation, but deliver us from evil;
For thine is the kingdom, and the power, and the glory,
Now and forever Father God,

"Father, you said in your Word that if we call on you and have the faith of a mustard seed, you would hear our cry. Father God, heal our sick sister's body and let the oxygen be able to flow throughout her body so she can be able to breathe normally again. It is in the Word and I have faith in you. You said it and I believe it."

The 23rd Psalm

The Lord is my shepherd: I shall not want.
He maketh me lie down in green pastures:
He leadeth me beside the still waters.
He restoreth my soul.
He leadeth me in the paths of righteousness for His name's sake.
Yea, though I walk through the valley of the shadow of death,
I will fear no evil: for thou art with me.
Thy rod and thy staff they comfort me.
Thou preparest a table before me in the presence of mine enemies;
Thou anointest my head with oil: my cup runneth over.
Surely, goodness and mercy shall follow me in all the days of my
life
And I will dwell in the house of the Lord forever. ***AMEN.***

Danielle felt the tears rolling down her cheeks as the weight started to lift up off her chest, and she could feel the energy coming from her husband's and brothers' bodies as they were praying. She felt the magic running through her veins and she was able to breathe almost normally. The pain went away. She thanked them for coming, and most of all, for their lovely prayers. She asked them to go home and get some rest; it was 3:00 a.m. She told them that she would be all right. She was receiving intermittent morphine intravenously and for break through pain, she was receiving a drug called Tordol intravenously.

The pain paralyzed her from her head to her toes. Danielle struggled to put her nurses' call light on, but she was unable to speak. When the nurse came to her room, she saw tears rolling down Danielle's cheeks and she went to get her some pain medication.

She must have drifted off to sleep and when she awakened, she glanced at her husband sitting over in the corner with his hands in the praying position.

"Napoleon, it is late," she said. "I want you to go home and get some sleep. I will be all right. She just wanted him to allow her the dignity to suffer alone. Danielle felt it was her fight and she had to go it alone. She sensed that a change was going to come. She had been born in a little house down on the river in Alabama, and she been running just like the river ever since.

There was a time when she felt as though she would not live this long. But she knew now that she could run on a little longer. She felt she had to have faith, and this too would pass. She felt she had to be strong so that her family could rest, and as time and change swirled around her, she, too, would be well again. She had so many things to live for. She believed she had the faith through trials and traumas and cares. She believed that she could handle this easily with wisdom and love. She felt that Jesus had cleared her vision and that now, she could see more clearly into the future for those around her as well as herself.

She felt that when she had an out-of-body experience, she did not die. It was her sins had died and she was reborn: "It is a new me," she thought. She felt that what had seemed like an out-of-body experience was, in reality, a door opening a new life, and God had given her a new gift of faith to tell this wonderful story. She felt God did not choose her because of her goodness, but because of her faith. It wasn't because of what she had done or not done that caused God to choose her. It was her faith in His promises as revealed in Jesus that lead her to obey Him.

She felt that God had chosen her not because she was perfect; He chose her because she had faith and believed in Him. She felt all of this would pass and that she would be well again.

The Caring Angel's

Sunday May 19, 7:00 a.m.

*T*he day nurse Heather, Registered Nurse, was making her morning rounds, she informed me that Dr. Cunningham was consulted and had ordered a V-Q scan to rule out a pulmonary embolism and she would be bringing a cardiac monitor to the department. She told Danielle that the transport was on its way.

Danielle asked the nurse to give her something for pain. A registered nurse helped her on the stretcher and took her through the corridors. It reminded her of the day she got married and the cars were all blowing their horns to let everyone know she and Napoleon had just gotten married with the sign "Just Married" on their car. Danielle felt this here as she went on a stretcher. The stretcher was all in white with a cardiac monitor and the nurse was letting everyone know she very ill.

Danielle just wanted to get rid of the constant pleuritic pain, coughing and wheezing, and to be able to breathe normally again. She arrived in the radiologist department for a V/Q scan. Tom Ross had this nice low-key voice and pleasant facial expression. He explained what he was about to do and he was joking around. He asked her how it felt to be the patient, instead of the nurse? Danielle smiled, whispering that she did not ask for this. She felt like she had been taken back through the tunnel of death. But this time, with her co-worker looking on and the radiologist.

The radiologist was as cheerful as the angel. He was looking through this large glass window, speaking through his income system. Danielle would wait to hear a cheerful voice saying "five more minutes."

She was taken back to her room, and shortly after, Dr. Gregory Cunningham came in and told her the V-Q scan was positive. There were tears rolling down her cheeks. He returned with her pain medication and told her he would wait until the pain was gone, and he sat in a chair beside her bed, wiping the tears from her eyes. He assured her that he would not leave her until he made her comfortable and free of pain. She must have fallen asleep and she noticed he had left, but shortly after, Dr. Cunningham returned to check on her and to make sure she was okay. Danielle felt that Dr. Gregory Cunningham was one of those Special Angels sent by Jesus to watch over and care for her.

She felt peace fullness come over her. In that instance, she knew that God was with her. She felt stronger and she knew she going to survive. It was encouraging to know that God cared about her safety and had sent Dr. Gregory Cunningham. Danielle recalled from her little black Bible reading as a child, "I will not leave you nor forsake you." She glanced over at Dr. Cunningham and she could see that glory mirrored in his face. She knew God stood right beside her. And she knew she was indeed in good hands, as she drifted back off to sleep.

God and his Angels Stood by

Monday, May 20

anielle felt she was very lucky to be alive after all that had happened to her.

She thanked Jesus for letting her see another birthday. Later that day, her family came and celebrated in her room with cake and ice cream. She felt a need to make a toast: "I thank God and His Angels for letting me see another birthday, and please let me breathe without pain. I would like to have a long, healthy, productive life." They all drank to that.

Danielle felt that Jesus had left her on earth for a reason. She learned in nursing school that we are our own worst enemies. If we take a negative attitude and a positive attitude, that equals a positive attitude. But if we take a negative and a negative, that equals a negative. So it does not take much to feel good about yourself. Danielle felt that nothing could stop her now. She would be the first to admit that yes, she felt depressed at times. But she refused to just give up and lie down and die. She knew that the only way she was going to get better was by thinking about the positive things in her life, especially her beautiful family.

Danielle knew she had to move away from herself and she began to think about her family's needs and how she could help them. She felt no blame toward Jesus or herself. She felt that if she was going to get better, it had to come from within her body, mind, and spirit.

Danielle started walking by faith. She felt that in this walk of faith, she would come to a crossroad and she would not know which way to turn, so she prepared herself for those difficult times by trusting in the Man above to help her along the way.

Danielle felt she had learned so much about herself that she had not known until the out-of-body experience touched her. She felt that when she had her first out-of-body experience, it was a message sent from Jesus to let her know that it was not time for her to die yet!! He said, "I just want to destroy your sins and I have given you a new life. There will be many doors open for you and you will see a change come. Therefore, my dear child, keep the faith in all you do.

Danielle felt that Jesus did not choose people because of their good or bad actions. She felt that when Jesus chose someone, it was because of his or her faith. She believed that all of the money, diamonds, and gold they had made no difference at all – it had no value where Jesus was concerned.

Danielle believed in his promise and his power. She felt that because of her faith, despite all of her ups and downs, God had chosen her so that she might teach someone else. She felt that Jesus did not choose one because of their wealth or non-wealth, nor did he choose anyone because of their good or bad actions. And, he did not choose one by their education of lack or education, nor by the color of his or her skin. Danielle felt that Jesus didn't see her as beautiful or ugly, young or old. He did not see black or white. She felt that Jesus' reason was a very simple one. You must have the desire, faith, and hope. She felt that no matter what happened, you just had to stand still. Danielle just lay still and waited for God.

There was times when she was unable to move her own body, and tears would be rolling down her cheeks. She would just lie still and continue to pray to God, feeling that eventually, the pain would ease up and she would be able to exchange her oxygen so she could breathe again.

Danielle felt nothing would stay the same forever, just like the seasons –winter, spring, summer and fall. The world itself is an axis, a real or an imaginary line on which the world rotates. She felt that we are somewhat like the axis: we have our good days when we are happy, and sometimes we are sad. Whatever the cause, we are no different than the axis of the world. She felt that just as the world has raindrops, we have our tears drops.

Danielle felt that Jesus would send a chosen person to take care of her when she needed someone, and she felt that Dr. Cunningham was that person when she needed a caring doctor. Dr. Gregory Cunningham was warm and had a caring heart. He reassured her with his knowledge and gifted hands. He made a diagnosis and treated her condition, with the right medications. The Heparin and Coumadin (Warfarin Sodium drug, USP) prevented more clots from forming and the morphine pain medication was able to float throughout her veins and ease her pain. As the PE. dissolved, her clinical picture gradually improved, without having a filter inserted into her arteries. And her combination anticoagulant levels were achieved. She was discharged on Warfarin. She was a little thinner, but she lived to tell her story.

It was very hard for her to be the patient in that bed, but the nurses, doctors and other staff members were expert, empathetic and diligent about keeping her informed of her status. She felt that she still had a long way to go, but she knew she could do it once she put her mind on the prize. Danielle worked hard in rehabilitation and recovered fully. She felt that God was the chief of her being. He sent Dr. Gregory Cunningham, who played a major role in her recovery and she made a friend for life. Her family and friends thank God and Dr. Cunningham for her life.

The Love for Mom

Never in a million years did Danielle ever think she would lose her mother and brother within eleven months of each other. Her mother had suffered from cancer for the past ten years and it took a toll on her body. In her last month before she crossed over, she had suffered with a great deal of pain and Danielle was there to the end.

Danielle is the splitting image of her mother, who was so beautiful and so sure of herself in everything she did. She felt she had a lot to be proud of.

Danielle will always remember her mother; she will forever be a special mother in her heart. One day, July 1, 1962 Danielle, felt so weak and had so little energy that she just could not get out of bed. She felt like she had the weight of the world on her shoulders. She wanted to go visit her mother that day, but she had to struggle to move around in the house. She called her sister Dee and told her she would not be visiting Mom that day, and said she had left the hospital around 2:00 a.m. She planned to stay home that day and would go visit Mom the next day. At times, her family put a lot of weight on her shoulders since she was the registered nurse in the family. As a registered nurse, they thought Danielle would take care of Mom or Dad and if they were ever sick, she would be there to give a helping hand. For the life of her family, they forgot that she was a person, too.

One of her brothers, Josha, called and told Danielle that their mother had pulled the suction tube out of her nose again and Danielle needed to come to the hospital and put it back in place. Their mother would not let the nurses put it back in her nose and Josha thought Danielle should come and see if their mother would let her insert it back in. Danielle asked Josha to tell their mom she would see her first thing the next morning; she was unable to make it that night.

Danielle told him she was not feeling well and was stressed out, rundown, and she needed some rest and sleep. Josha continued to tell her that she should come now and he would pay her. She told Josha that it was not about money; her body was tired and burned out. Tears ran down her cheeks as she spoke. Napoleon overheard

Danielle talking to her brother. He told her he would carry her in his arms.

"Napoleon, you and Josha just do not understand," Danielle told him. I can't take it anymore. I can feel Mom's pain. When Mom hurts, I hurt, too, and I feel so bad because I am unable to help her. I know I am a registered nurse, but what good is that now? I am unable to help the one person who gave birth to me and took care of me, when I could not care for myself. With all the new medication and research, cancer is destroying our mom. Please tell her I will see her early tomorrow morning."

Danielle just needed a little rest. She would be all right in the morning.

She got out of bed at around 5:00 a.m., feeling stronger and she had this instinct –a feeling came over her, and, as she was walking out the door, she heard the phone ringing. Napoleon called her to tell her that her mother was very critical. Danielle told Napoleon that her mother had been critical for months.

Napoleon said the nurse would not call for no reason and that he would go to the hospital with her. Danielle felt that her mother had crossed over and the nurse was protecting her as much as possible.

On July 2, 1992, at 6:00 a.m., the nurse called back from the hospital telling Danielle that her worst nightmare was now a reality. Her mother had crossed over to be with Danielle's father in heaven.

Danielle felt very upset and guilty because she was not there. She prayed to Big Brother to please forgive her, because she was not there with her mother when she died. Danielle prayed that someday she would be able to see her mother and tell her face-to-face, in heaven. She just wanted to tell her that she loved her and was so upset because she was not there when her mother needed her most. Then, Danielle felt this calm feeling come over her. The Angels had kept her home so her daddy could come and take her mother back to Heaven with him. Her brother Joseph whispered those comforting words into her ear because she was so distraught at their mother's funeral. It took her a few years to find peace within her self.

Daniel's mother died two months before her birthday. She was born on September 2, and crossed over on July 2, 1992. On June 23, 1993, Father Day's, at around twelve midnight, Danielle received a chilling phone call. When she answered the phone, she heard someone crying and at first, she could not understand what the person was saying. Then she realized that it was her younger brother's girlfriend, Jennifer, on the phone, telling Danielle that her brother was having a heart attack, and she was trying to help him.

Mark crossed over on June 23, 1993, two months before his birthday, August 23. Her brother was handsome, with a young, tall, lean body build, six-feet-four inches. His weight was normal for his size. He ate the right kind of foods, exercised, and had his own small business training people how to eat healthily, exercise and lose weight. He did not drink nor use recreational drugs, and his family still finds it hard to swallow. Danielle still cannot believe that Mark is no longer with them.

Our Brother Our Hero

anielle still can see her brother Mark's face when they were all standing around their mother's bed crying after their mother had crossed over to the other side. Mark leaned over their mother and softly whispered in her ear that she was not going to leave him behind like Daddy did. He kissed her on the forehead and said he would be joining her soon and he walked away crying.

Mark had been very upset with his ex-wife for not letting him bring their children to see their grandmother, who had been asking to see the kids, and he felt so helpless that he could not give their mother the one thing she wanted before she crossed over. He felt sad about her leaving him; the love only a mother can give to her son was all gone now, too. Mark felt he had neither a mother nor kids to call his own.

Brothers are very special. Sometimes we do not tell someone that we care about him or her and love him or her. Even though our hearts are filled with love, we keep all of our feelings buried deep down inside of us. With a brother, this can be so true.

But, Danielle hopes that her brother Mark knew that he meant a lot to the family because he really did, and not a day goes by that she doesn't think about him. She can still see his nice white teeth and big beautiful smile.

Things have not been the same on Father's Day without Mark, but Danielle tries to cope with the memories of the thirty-four years he was with her family. She would like nothing more than to have him back home, coaching her on how to lose weight and encouraging her never to give up – "You can do it."

She misses having him here to make her laugh and to listen to him sing like Berry White. He always had a sense of what to do when the chips were down to make her feel better by telling a joke just to make someone smile.

Danielle took acting classes in the Big Apple and when she was unable to find her way around the city, she would talk to Mark, who had crossed over, just as if he was right there walking beside her. Danielle looked over her left side and then up at the sky, and the funny thing was that she could feel his presence right beside her leading the way. Before she knew it, she was exactly at the place she was looking for.

Danielle knew that when she was on that stage acting, she never missed a cue and she really enjoyed being in front of the spotlight. She remembered that she was very shy; she would never get up and talk in front of folks she did not know. But now, Mark brought out the very best in her. She made the folks laugh and forget about their problems for the moment.

Danielle said to Mark, "I now know you live on and that makes me strong. You know, the strangest thing is that when one door closes, another one opens. Brother, I must tell you this. One day, I followed this man who looked and walked just like you, all around in the store. I approached him and told him he looked so much like my brother. He just said 'thank you" and walked away. And then, there was this young man who sounded just like you at work. One day, I heard his voice and I turned around and thought it was you. Oh, what I would give just to see you and talk to you again. Sometimes, I put my hair up and wear a baseball cap and I can see you through my eyes. I will never forget the time I gave you this big "Happy Birthday" balloon and all of a sudden, a whirlwind came along and took it away from me. At first I was upset and then I thought to myself it was you who came and took it away and it went straight up into the sky and on up to heaven. I smiled and walked away."

Danielle felt relief now; her brother Mark was going back to see Mother and Dad and the rest of her family. Danielle told her brother that she would miss him always. She would never stop loving him, and she would always remember the brother who always knew what to say when the chips were down. She said to him, "I will see you in Heaven one day. Say Hello to Mom and Dad and the rest of the family. My dearest brother, I still love you!!"

Danielle felt that if she stopped loving her little brother, then she would have to face the fact that Mark was truly dead and gone forever. She would never see his smiling face again. She believed that if she continued to love him, it would be like he would be back. She felt that was the only way she would be able to survive from day to day with her own life. She had been struggling to keep her weight down and there were a few rolls here and there. She missed her brother coaching and encouraging her to workout every morning and every night before she went to bed. She felt that she had to think of the fun things they did growing up in Alabama.

Danielle could still see her little brother's face the first time she went back to Alabama to visit her family after she moved to New Jersey. She remembered when she was packing her luggage – one of those old-fashioned cardboard suitcases with this green satin-silk material inside and a shiny buckle on the outside. Mark would get into this suitcase and hide under her clothes. She would never forget one day when her mom was looking for her brother and found him inside Danielle's suitcase. He was hiding there so he could go back to New Jersey with Danielle.

Her brother Mark will always be close to her heart and she will never forget him and that big handsome smile, and bright white teeth. She looked up to the sky and said, "Brother, I will love you forever, and we miss you so much!!!

Seeing Through a Childs's Eyes

*H*er earliest memory is of herself as a three-year-old. Her mama had just finished combing her long hair and had instructed her to go outside and play. As Danielle was running out the front door, she spotted the most beautiful little girl staring back at her from the large standing looking glass. The girl followed Danielle around, but she would not play with her. Danielle ran back into the house and asked Mama if it was okay for her to play with the little girl. But Mama simply smiled and replied, "Danielle, you are the only little girl in the house and you should just go out and play with your toys." Undeterred, Danielle stubbornly stomped out of the room, determined to prove to Mama that there was indeed another little girl there. Danielle went back to the mirror, but when she ran behind it to catch up with the little girl, the child was gone. This happened time and time again that day until, exhausted, she ran to her room, crying, and fell asleep. *Why wouldn't that little girl come out and play with me?* Danielle wondered. She thought the little girl was so pretty.

It didn't take Mama long to figure out exactly what was going on. She plopped Danielle on her raised knees, her nose level with her shapely eyebrows, frowning fiercely at her little serious face, and tried to explain to her that she was that little girl in the mirror. Danielle didn't believe Mama. Her two older sisters even tried to convince that she was only a shadow and that the other girl was actually herself – Danielle – and that was why she could not come out and play.

Danielle was so confused. The child in the mirror was a beautiful high-yellow and skinny little girl with long brown hair. She had big round eyes set deep in a large, round, pudgy little face. Danielle looked at her two sisters, both of who were darker than the girl in the mirror. She had always just assumed she was the same color as they. But she was not. Her sisters' skin was the color of deep coffee; Danielle's was closer to that of caramel candy. As a young child, Danielle did not yet understand, or even see, the difference in their skin colors.

Racism is a learned response, not an inherited one. Until that day, she saw all people as being the same. Black, White, Indian, Hispanic, Asian – skin color did not matter. But she was a black child, seeing things through a child's eyes, growing up in the Deep South, and she felt that once we are born, our autonomic nervous system takes over and controls the vital function that sustains life. A metronome by the will of a Higher Power keeps our heart beating, our lungs breathing, and our blood circulating; we have no control over it. Danielle believed that we have nothing to say about who lives and who dies; humans have no control over who gets a certain disease and who doesn't. No man should think he is better than the other person, because the same Man placed us all on this earth, whether we like it or not. But in the South, that did not hold true. In the South, folks' attitudes were just like a great big puzzle that reached from north, west, east, and south.

Danielle felt as she was exploring that she learned many things about herself and her family's history. Her father's grandfather was born to a black woman and a white man. At an early age, he was taken out of his mother's arms, and was reared by white people, and used as a slave until he became free. She never knew his biological parents. Her mother and grandfather were half-Indian and his biological parents raised him. Her parents had fourteen children in all; two sets of twin boys were stillborn. Her oldest brother died at age four, and so did her second-eldest sister.

Danielle felt that Alabama was a very hot and dry state, and the small towns were broken down into minorities; about one-third lived in poverty, a rate three times higher than that of the white population. Most of the poor lived in areas typical of poverty; poor, overcrowded – crowded schools and crowded housing. Most of the people worked as sharecroppers.

As for her family, they lived in their great-grandfather's home and they had their own land, over one hundred and eighty acres. There were poor white people and there were the upper-class whites. The large sections of the cities looked clean and shiny, as if they had been built a few days before. All the white folks would speak to you, but some were nasty, while there were others who were nice and friendly. Her dad's white friends seemed to be very nice and pleasant to talk with and they would do anything for him. Most surprising of all, a majority of the white folks would speak to you if they met you in the street; for example, "good morning" or "good afternoon" or "hi, how ya all doing?" Danielle felt that if they liked you, they liked you and if they did not, they would let you know that, too.

She felt that they would not laugh in your face and stab you in the back, like some of the northern white folks. Her mama told her that they could get beaten up if they were to drink water from a fountain where there was a sign with "White" written on it, rather than the one with "Colored" written on it. As a child, she was unable to read that, but her parents taught her how to know the difference between the two at an early age. The letter "C" meant colored folks and the "W" meant white folks. Mama said they were colored. Danielle said, "Look at this crayon. I thought you said this is white, but the white folks do not look like this, do they, Mama? They are pinkish, yellow-looking folks, aren't they, Mama? They are colored, too, aren't they, Mama?"

"Now you listen up, child. Don't be hardheaded. They think they are white and that's what they've called themselves for hundreds of years. White folks called us colored folks, nigger folks, and some called us black folks. When they call us "nigger," they are trying to put you down, saying we aren't worth anything. But you listen up, dear child. You are just as good as that white boy or white girl. You are somebody. Keep your head up high, baby girl, and don't fall into their traps. If they call us Negroes, I can respect that, but anything else, no, no, no! If it says 'Colored folks,' that means you can use it. You must never use anything when it has 'Whites' wrote on it."

Well, what's wrong with our color? Danielle thought to herself. As a child, she could not understand what the big fuss was about, of misery about drinking from the wrong water fountain or using the same outhouse with "White" written on it. Danielle just didn't understand. Niggers, colored, blacks, browns, yellows, greens, blues. She was so confused. She thought that's what you called colors. She felt this was just a lot of jumbled, jabber-talk.

"Who came up with this silly stuff anyway? Danielle asked. "It is not in the Bible, is it, Mom"?

"No, child. Now go on."

66

"Oh"…"

"Ah, what did you say?"

"Nothing, Mama."

"Now you just put all of that on the back burner for now – but don't turn it off."

"Just keep it in the back of my head, Mama?"

"Yes, child, and in the long run, this will help you find solutions to many problems, and this way, you won't have to get yourself all worked up."

She felt she had to run this one off, so she ran out the door singing, "Sticks and stones may break my bones, but talk won't ever hurt me." Now Danielle could see it all in the eyes of oneself.

Dreams Do Come True Forever

The love Danielle and Napoleon shared stood in the midst of their lives. It was bold and beautiful. They felt they had a place in the world that was unique. A path to walk that was theirs alone. Danielle felt she had the spirit that was bold and bright, and the caring to create. She had so many dreams to seek. No matter what, she knew that she must keep her wits about her. Danielle stopped and thought about where they had been, and dreamed about where they were going.

American Dream

anielle wondered, is the old rags-to-riches fable of the American Dream still feasible in a time when violence, AIDS, child, spouse abuse, divorce, teenage pregnancy, drugs, and gang wars consume our nation?

As a child, she was taught to believe that if she wanted something badly enough, she could obtain it. Grown-up now, though, she realized that this is not always the case. Wishing does not always make it so. If we are lucky, we were taught that we must be willing to work to achieve our dreams. Danielle was taught that no amount of failure should deter her from her goals. The ambition is the driving force that makes it all come together.

By being hardworking, persistent and ambitious, Danielle has achieved her own version of this American Dream. She has always been a very hard working individual. As a youngster, she worked long hours on the family farm carrying bushels of cotton from the fields, milking cows and assisting in the care of her younger siblings. As an adult, she worked twelve-hour shifts as a nurses' aide, all the while raising two children, and going to school full-time to obtain a registered nursing degree. Yet she could always find the time to attend every single one of her son's soccer and baseball games. She never missed a PTA meeting at school. In fact, it wasn't uncommon to see her sitting in the bleachers cheering at a game with her notebook in her hand, so she could also re-read the day's class notes.

There were times, though, when the delicate balancing act of hers caused her to fail one of her per- tests at school. When this happened, she became even more persistent in achieving her goals. She saw that a failed per-test was a learning experience from her mistakes and she passed her main tests. Often, this would mean long nights of study even after working at the hospital all day, and she would play her tape recorder while she slept. Danielle remembered telling her brother that the brain is just like a computer; all you have to do is to record your thoughts and when you needed the information, it would recall the answer you needed. Eventually, one by one, she passed all her tests and graduated.

None of this would have been possible, though, if she did not have an immense amount of ambition as her primary driving force. When she originally started college, her main objective was to become a licensed practical nurse. However, instead she decided to go for her registered nurse. registered nurse. A couple of years later, she graduated. Even as she walked down the aisle, she had already decided to continue her education and once again returned to school for her Bachelor Of Science Degree in Nursing. However, as she was working on her, Master's Degree, she were struck down in a serious car accident.

Yes, even though our nation is in the midst of many crises, it is still possible to achieve the American Dream of success. However, it requires more from us than simply being in the right place at the right time. Nor is it a matter of just winning a couple of million dollars in a lottery. Danielle has emphasized this dream in her lifetime. She had evolved from an innocent country girl to a diligent professional nurse. She applied the principles of hard work, persistence, and good old-fashioned ambition to show that it is indeed possible to come from a great-grandfather of a slave to a rather humble being and to soar to the very top.

There Is No Failure

anielle believes that there is no failure; there is only a delay in results. She believes that one must not even dismiss or nullify good, positive energy because you are disappointed. Acquire the attitude, and have patience. It really does wonders for you in your body, mind, and well-being.

Danielle felt that one of the tenets of neurolingeuistic programming is that there is no such thing as failure; only feedback and patience is power.

When she sees a rainbow flash across the sky, its brilliant rays in the light blue sky in shades of yellow, orange, peach, pink, red, lavender, and purple, cause her to believe that it is God's way of saying, "Look at how beautiful life can be and all things are possible if you put just a little faith in me."

She thanks God for all the rainbow colors in the sky and the bright sunny days. Even though sometimes it may be raining or snowing, Danielle still looks on the bright side of life because it is the colors that remind her of God's love for us, with the earth He created: the earth and trees, which are nice and green; the blue ocean water and the seas; the white sand on the beaches, and the white clouds in the sky. Danielle feels that is God's way of saying that this is purity and when a man and woman come together in marriage, the bride always wears a white gown or a white dress. She feels it when she sees the strips of red in the rainbows. Danielle believes that this is God's way of showing us how He shed his blood and died on the cross so that we may be free. She feels that the darkness of day was His death. Danielle sometimes thinks back and wonders why some men wear black when they get married. She feels that black is death and the darkness and the grayest day in our lives when our loved one crosses over into a new world. She believes that it is not about the colors a person wears; it is about the feelings they have in their heart and what they believe in.

Danielle feels that when she goes to work from sunrise to sundown, she is stuck. Inside those cold stone walls, working in the hospital caring for patients, with all kinds of health problems, from the very young to the very old, she feels that each person is unique in his or her own way, and she asks God to please give her the knowledge and the strength to meet all her patients' needs, demands, and she wants to give each and every one the kind of care they so desire to the best of her ability. Danielle knows all too well what it like being a patient in that bed.

She feels that when she walks into her patients' rooms, she has to bring in the sunshine. She greets each of her patients with respect and with a burst of sunshine by giving them a big smile, and saying, "Good morning. How are you today? How was your night?" Now some may say, "What is so good about it?" Some of her patients may say they had a bad night, and Danielle wants to know how she can make the patient's day better. She lets them know that she is there for them. She aims to please.

As she walks out of their rooms, she looks down those long, dark corridors and tries to remember what it was like when she emerged into the fresh air, and was greeted by the stars and the moon that light up the black sky as she sits in her car trying to unwind. She feels her spirit lift as God refreshes her, and that beautiful sensation throughout for her special time of communication with God.

An Angel Message

very night Danielle prayed for her family and especially for her daughter who was only seventeen and already away at college, living on her own in a dormitory room. She often talked about having to eat vegetable lasagna, without any meat, and how bad it tasted, and many times she would not eat until the next day. Or, she would pick up some fast food at a place near the college.

Danielle's daughter, Melissa, is 5 feet, five inches tall, and weighs about 105 pounds soaking wet. Although Melissa is small, she is very strong and has a good head on her shoulders. And, she is very determined about her education.

She would always complain about flying back and forth to Chicago every weekend, and how she had to take three subways to get back to the college. Danielle felt tired just listening to Melissa talk about everything she had to go through to come home.

Danielle was awakened during the night by a spirit that came to tell her that her daughter was not doing well, and the spirit said Danielle would receive a phone call in which the caller would say, she had some good news and some not so good news. This was around 3:00 a.m. She did not fall back to sleep for the rest of the night. She was tossing and turning all night long. Finally, daylight came and she was lying there praying for her daughter to call home, and hoping she was okay.

As Danielle lay there daydreaming about her life, a memory of something that happened to her as a little girl flashed before her eyes and really bothered her. She was thinking about when she was a young child and got sick and almost died, and how frightened she was when she woke up, and now her poor teenage daughter was sick and she was not there for her.

It was very cold that day and the weatherman was predicating snow and they already had God knew how much snow on the ground. Danielle felt she had to be strong and of good courage, and not be afraid of the weather for God was watching over her. He would not leave her nor forsake her. It was in his "Word "and she trusted and believed in him. She just had to be strong for her family's sake.

Finally, daylight came and she was lying there praying for her daughter to call and tell her everything was all right. All of a sudden, Danielle thought she heard the phone ring and she could hear that something was wrong by the tone of her daughter's voice. She had been having a dream that it was raining. She grabbed the phone, but no one was on it. Danielle started to call Melissa, but in order for her to speak with her, someone from the security department at the front desk would have to send someone up five flights of stairs to wake her up.

The college did not have phones in the room at the time, and Danielle did not want to bother anyone if Melissa was all right. Finally, the phone rang early in the morning, and she grabbed the phone again and this time, she heard a voice plainly say, "Mom I have some good new and some not so good news." "What's wrong, Melissa?"

She said she had passed most of her examinations and had two more to take. Danielle said, "Wait! Wait!" She jumped out of bed yelling for her to wait a minute. Danielle had been sleeping and she thought she was dreaming. She ran into the bathroom to look into the mirror and wash her face, to make sure she was not asleep. Her husband yelled, "What is the matter?" and grabbed the phone out of her hand. "Okay, are you all right?" Danielle picked up the other phone. She was listening to her daughter's heart beating a hundred miles a minute It was so loud that it pulsed against her eardrums. Her poor daughter continued to explain that she would be all right. "But I'm really sick," she said, "and I do not remember the last time I ate some food. I have a sore throat and have been eating soap for the past three days." Her throat was sore and she thought she had a temperature, and she would try to go to the doctor sometime next week and see if he would give her an antibiotic because she had been sick now for about two weeks, and she just couldn't shake this cold. She said she was going to take two Tylenol and go back to bed and rest all day. She assured Danielle that she was all right. But deep down inside, Danielle knew that she was not all right and that she needed to have an antibiotic on board. Danielle could hear the trembling as she talked with her dad. Melissa said she loved them and hung up the phone. Tears started rolling down Danielle's cheeks as she lay there thinking about the "what if?"

Danielle jumped up and told Napoleon that she was going to Chicago to take care of their daughter. Napoleon said, "I think you should go. What time do you want to leave for the airport?" "Yesterday!!!" said Danielle.

Danielle told him she would call Melissa's doctor first, but the office did not open until 9:00 a.m. "I will inform the doctor that Melissa is sick with a very bad cold and has been for about two weeks and she needs cough syrup and antibiotics. Napoleon, you can make my reservation for a 12:00 o'clock flight today to Chicago."

Danielle raced downstairs, packed her overnight bag and dressed in warm cloths for her trip. Dr. John Holliday called back and she told him her daughter had been sick for about two weeks and was complaining of a sore throat and chills and she needed some antibiotics. Her throat tightened and she had a problem getting the words through her lips. Danielle tried to tell him what had happened. He said he would call in the prescription to the drugstore right away. His voice was calmer than Danielle's and that comforted her. Danielle was starting to feel better now. At least she had some medication for her daughter and she would be taking it to her today.

Napoleon went to pick up the medication while Danielle finished dressing and went to the bank. She felt that her son should stay home just in case her daughter called her back and he would let her know that Danielle was on her way to visit her and she was bringing her some medications.

Danielle and Napoleon both arrived back home at the same time and Danielle ran inside the house, got her bag and headed out to the airport. It was 10:00 a.m. and her flight would leave at noon. She was about an hour and a half away on a good day with not too much traffic, and today was Saturday. Who knew how much traffic would be going to the airport on a Saturday, and God only knew how many accidents there would be on the turnpike.

It was very cold out, but thank God the sun was shining. Danielle felt as if her heart was racing about one hundred and sixty beats a minute. They were about halfway to the airport and Napoleon looked over at her and asked if she had any directions for where she was going once she got to Chicago. She said she didn't have the slightest clue. Napoleon said, "So how are you going to find our daughter?" Danielle said, "I am going to pray to God to help me find her." Napoleon looked at her as if he did not hear her, or believe her. He said, "What did you say?" Danielle told him to let her think for a minute. She felt she had to close her eyes, and she asked God to help her find her daughter who was sick and Danielle had no clue where to go once she arrived in Chicago.

Then all of a sudden, her New Brain jumped into the driver's seat, saying, "You will find her." Danielle started to remember that every weekend when her daughter came home, she would be complaining about the three subways she had to take when she would get off the plane to get back to the college. There were times she, herself, would get lost and missed her stops.

She would be talking about how she had to get off the A-subway and take it to Hope: Street and then she would take the C-subway to 145 -street and then take a B-subway to 160th West Street, get off the subway and walk up eight flights of stairs and she would be about four blocks from the college. She would just keep walking west. Danielle had no idea she would be traveling in the same direction as Melissa did. She felt that Angels have many ways of reaching out, but sometimes we might miss them. There are times when you pick up a book and a page might fall open with a clear message in the print. Danielle would take a special notice of that page and read it. She knew that there are also times a message would appear to her in a dream. Danielle felt that Angels are very creative in the ways they get their message across to us. And we need to be just as creative when we listen for their messages. She felt very sure that an angel was traveling with her to locate her daughter at college. Danielle had no feeling of fear, nor did she have any anxiety. She felt that the Angels were speaking to her through her thoughts, and she did not have to do anything fancy nor did she have to be at one of the holy grounds. All she had to do was to trust herself, think positively and have a self-love attitude and be kind in her thoughts and actions. Danielle felt the Angels loved her unconditionally.

She asked God to build a fence around her and let His light shine on her just like the blood flowing through her body. She knew that it was an angel because they did not leave her confused, and the message was clear.

The Angel Leads the Way

anielle felt that the brain works like a computer and when you click on your mouse on certain items you are trying to locate, it will come into play. She felt she needed to bring her computer brain into focus, so she put her hand on a pen and started to write wherever her mind led her and about all the directions her daughter had talked about when she came home. Melissa had told her several time before, but Danielle hadn't really been listening to her. Melissa complained about coming home, every time she had the chance. She never wrote the directions down. Danielle closed her eyes and imagined she was going back home and she got an intuitive sense to come into focus. She was able to pick up her daughter's emotional feeling of going back home.

Danielle wrote down every single direction that Melissa had told her – about how she would take the subways to go back to the college and how she really did not like doing that.

Danielle opened her eyes and began to write all of her directions down on a piece of paper. She looked over at her husband and told him she had her directions now, and she remembered every single subway number and every single street number and said she would find their daughter.

Danielle arrived in Chicago around 1:00 p.m. She picked up her bag and went straight to the subways. She got on the right one and got off at the right numbers and streets without making a single mistake, nor did she have to ask a single person for directions. She just followed the ones she had written down. Danielle went to the college security doorman and one of the security people took her up to her daughter's room. She knocked on Melissa's door and said it was Mom.

Melissa she said "Who?"

Danielle repeated, "Mom," and Melissa opened the door. She was in a state of shock to see Danielle standing at the door.

"Now, Mother, how did you get here so fast?"

Danielle told her she had taken a plane and then walked down to the subway."

Melissa couldn't believe this. "And you did not get lost?" she asked.

"No." Danielle assured Melissa that this was not her doing; but that the Angels had led the way and she followed them.

Melissa had to sit down. Danielle showed her the directions she had written down on this small piece of paper, and Melissa checked it and said, "I cannot believe this. These directions are perfect, Mom."

Danielle smiled and said, "You know, Melissa, God does not make mistakes and He will always help His children when they are in need. All you have to do is call Him and He will take care of you."

Danielle felt that trials are like beautiful multiple-color blooming roses. The stem is long and coved with sharp thorns; at the end are a crowning flower and that flower represented not only the blessings of patiently abiding in God, but also the blessing we will receive. Afterwards, we jumped for joy.

Mom and Dad

anielle felt that her parents were very special; they gave her the tools she needed to build on in her life and the knowledge she needed to use them successfully. They gave her the courage to overcome obstacles, and the confidence she needed in her everyday life and in nursing school. Her father told her repeatedly to take pride in a job well done. She felt her parents gave her the living steppingstone of excellence to follow, as a child, woman and as a mother.

She was blessed with parents who followed God, so that their children could learn and grow – unselfish parents who held on with love and yet they knew when it was time to let go. Danielle felt she had the kind of parents whose faith kept them going, through all their trials, and who grew in wisdom and love.

Danielle felt she was blessed with the type of vision that met all her needs, from the first day she was born. She believed that she was blessed with the type of parents who shared her love for God and His special Angels on earth. She felt she had to be a special kind of mother to set a course in life for her children and follow through, no matter what the obstacles. She felt she had to be a special kind of mother like her mother – which she, too, had to be the best, and to pursue her goals with passion, love, and enthusiasm.

She felt she had to be a special kind of mother like her mother whose faith, inspiration and determination led to admiration and whose perseverance always made her a winner. Danielle felt that she had to be that special kind of parent, too.

Being Strong:

anielle felt as she looked back over her life that she was not perfect. She had made her share of mistakes too. Everyone makes mistakes, but it is the smart person who admits that she has made mistakes. She felt that a mistake was a learning tool that one can build on and that makes them a better person. God did not make a perfect person; if He did, He would have nothing to teach them.

If you think you are perfect, maybe you need to do a mental assessment of yourself. Danielle had her ups and downs, struggling to grow up, in the deep south of Alabama. She felt that she wanted to make the present better than her past. She felt she had to take on a new role in her life and do things differently, so she started to plan for her future, and the only way she could do that was to adopt a positive attitude.

Danielle felt she needed to come to terns with herself, her past and moving to a new understanding with herself. She became more aware of who she was and where she had been. Danielle felt she had to be strong in the power of the Lord, and the almighty God. She felt she had to take a stand against the wiles and wrestle not against principles, but against powers – against the rules and regulations of the darkness of the world and she felt like she was in a spiral down low.

Danielle felt she had to be strong so that others could rest, as time and change swirled around then. She felt she had to focus on the here and now, for the love she shared stood quietly in the midst of her life. Forever beautiful. She stopped, and thought about where she had been and what she had dreamed about, and where she was going. She felt that in all the good times and all the trying times, she would forever have a friend who would never leave her, and his name was Big Brother.!!!

A Sister's Love

anielle felt that a sister is life's special friend. Her sister, Dee, played a special part in her life and memories forever. Dee would forever be special in her heart. Danielle felt there could never be a sister lovelier than her sister could. Danielle had such special moments with her sister. She will always remember their times, growing up. She will treasure the times from her past.

When Danielle was two years old, every time her dad would go to work, she would cry all day until he come home, and her mother would spank her to try to make her stop crying. Dee was so special. She would take Danielle to the road and wait for Dad to come back home in all of that hot sun. It took a special sister to care for her then and to care for her now.

Danielle feels very, very grateful to have a special sister like Dee to care for now.

Danielle loved her growing-up days, but the years flew by so fast. She felt she wanted to be like her sister. She would take her clothes and wear her hair on top of her head just like Dee

When Danielle was sick, she would call Dee and she took care of Danielle. She was a sister whom Danielle could depend on, no matter what. She came and combed her hair when she was unable to lift up her arm. When she was so weak and unable to stand, Dee was there. What a special sister, loving, caring, and thoughtful.

All the love they found growing up is something Danielle will cherish forever. Dee is her sister and best friend, too.

Angel Glowing

One day Danielle was sitting in the park thinking about her life and trying to figure out where she went wrong, and what she had done right. She felt she had more problems than Carter has mustard seeds.

Danielle noticed the ducks in the pond of water and how each one followed the mother. The baby ducks all seemed very happy, following their mother, and here Danielle was sitting there all alone.

Danielle had tried to walk in her mother's footsteps before she died, and she, too, was very happy when her mother was alive, and now she had her good days and her bad days. Danielle tried to live in the present and look to the future, but she felt herself starting to drift back into the past. As she was sitting there feeling sorry for herself, Danielle heard this shuffling sound coming down the sidewalk from behind. She glanced over her left shoulder and noticed an old woman all bent over, pushing her walker down the sidewalk.

The woman looked over at Danielle and asked, "Do you mind if I sit down here for a few minutes to rest? I'm a little tired." Danielle said she would be delighted for her to sit down. She told the woman that she came there every day just to watch the ducks in the water and it was very relaxing for her.

As the old woman sat there resting, she looked over at Danielle and said, "You poor child. You seem like you are troubled about something. And what happened to your leg and shoulder? I see you have a crutch over there. Danielle told her that she had a car accident last year and it left her all broken up. She had a lot of pain at times. She refused take pain medications, because, she said, "They will control you if you let them and I want control over my own life. And they will drive you crazy. But today is a good day. The sun is shinning and I guess I'm feeling a little sorry for myself today. But I will be all right." Danielle was watching the ducks in the water and how they were following their mother. She told the woman that she had lost her mother a few years before to cancer, and her mother had suffered very badly. Danielle said she had done everything she could to make it easy for her mother, but she just could not do enough.

The old woman placed her hands on Danielle's hand and said, "My dear child, try to remember the good days with your mother and she will always be alive as long as she is in your heart, and every time you think about her smile. When you smile, she smiles, too. And when you feel sad and cry, she cries, too. So just smile when you are happy and smile when you are sad and you will live a very long time. Just look at me. I will be 90 years old on my next birthday. Do you see that old gray house up the street? I have lived there all my life. At one time, it was full of my family and now I'm the only one living there. I have no one but myself.

Are you married?" she asked Danielle. She told the woman "Yes." "Do you have children?" asked the woman. "Oh, yes, I have two, but they both live out of town," said Danielle.

The old woman told Danielle that she had gotten married at an early age. And her husband was in the army and when she became pregnant with her second child, he was killed and he never got the chance to see his son. Their daughter was just two-years-old at the time. She lost her daughter to cancer about ten years ago. Her son had been a policeman and he was coming out of the store where this man was being robbed at gunpoint. Her son was trying to help him and he got shot in the chest and died a few hours later. The owner of the store was also injured, but he lived long enough to tell the story; he died two days later. They picked up the gunman and he were jailed for life.

The old woman was all alone, and one day while she was sitting down in a chair at her table, writing out her bills, she felt her face start to twitch. Her right hand started to shake and she was unable to stop them. She thought she was having a diabetic reaction. The woman said to herself that she had just eaten her dinner so this could not be happening to her. She stood up to reach for the phone on the table and she must have pulled the table down on top of herself and hit her head. The phone fell on the floor and she was not able to get it. The woman said she must have passed out. Finally, she woke up, but she was unable to move her right side and she had blood on her head. She was lying there for hours, struggling, trying to reach the phone and keep her wits about her.

The lady began praying to God to help her. She felt that God often worked in us through life's discomforts and challenges and could change our attitudes toward them. As the lady was struggling, she began to look around to see God. She started to see that her struggling became not walls, not sickness, but doors; not obstacles, but bridges. The lady started dragging her body along the floor, and finally, she was able to reach the phone and call the operator. The operator called 911 for her, and the paramedics came and took her to the hospital. She was in the rehabilitation center for about eight months. She worked hard to gain strength in her right leg. Her right arm still didn't have the strength she hoped for. Her doctors said she would never get any better. The lady said it was a struggle to use her walker and she no longer could drive her car. She had poor vision too. A nurse came out to her house a few days a week to help her out and stayed for a few hours. She said she felt very blessed to have someone to care for her at her age because it was hard to get good help nowadays.

The Voice Of Angels

*J*oy and happiness are as much a part of life as sunrise and sunset. However, the mere mention of two words causes us to bristle and feel uneasy at best. Napoleon was born on a Friday, the 13th. When a baby is born, we as parents consider nothing but joy, but when we face trials and tribulations, this seems to some of us to be a bad luck day and contrary to our human nature.

On September 30, 2002, Danielle received a phone call from one of her dearest friends – a registered nurse from work. They had worked together for over twenty years and their birthdays were just one day apart, and the two registered nurses have celebrated their birthdays together one way or another for the past twenty years. So now, how could she tell her best friend, Lisa, that she would not be able to come to her daughter's wedding, without hurting her feelings, and ruining their relationship? And this friend's husband had walked out on her and the children years before. She depended on Danielle and her husband being there.

Danielle did not want to take away the joy from her friend and her friend's daughter. Lisa was very excited to tell Danielle the great news that her daughter was getting married, and she wanted Danielle and her husband to come to the wedding, on December 13th, on a Friday night. Danielle told Lisa that she didn't think she had heard her right. Lisa repeated it again.

"Your daughter is getting married on December 13, Friday night?" Lisa yes, "You know your granddaughter, Ronda, the one who, when you came to the hospital to see her and the nurse said only mothers and grandmother could visited, you looked her straight in the face and said, 'Well, I guess that makes me a grandmother.'? Danielle felt there were walls between a husband and wife, parent and child, and friend and friend. There are

walls of silence, walls of self, walls of words and walls and walls. There are times when we try to talk to someone new and walls begin to arise. But, this registered nurse friend did not hold anything back. She had some good news to tell Danielle, and no matter what, she was going to tell her. This friend of hers would knock the wall down to get her point across to her. Danielle felt she had to stop and listen and hear the nice things, but who pauses to listen, here or any place else?

There was no way Danielle could talk Lisa out of having the wedding on Friday 13th. Danielle believed it was a bad luck day —an old wives' tale. She felt that Angels speak to us, but at times we do not hear them because we do not recognize them —Angel voices aimed at the negatives in our lives. If we are not listening to the positive, we will not hear when Angels speak.

A few weeks before the wedding, Napolean and Danielle went up north to the Woodbridge New Jersey Mall, just to do a little window-shopping. Needless to say, her husband spotted a suit that caught his eye and he decided to go into the store and try it on. The suit looked like it was made for him and they bought it. Napoleon fitted for the slacks and they told him he could pick up the suit in three days, which was on a Wednesday before the wedding.

After the fitting, Napoleon was complaining about feeling weak and he wanted to go and have some lunch. After they ate, he said he felt better and soon afterwards, they decided to come home. As they were coming down the parkway, Danielle began to try to piece things together about how he was feeling. Now, here was a tall, lean man, who never had experienced this type of problem in the past. Danielle told him she could understand that he was trying to lose weight by cutting back on how much he ate. But he should be gaining energy instead of losing energy.

Napoleon said, "Yes, I thought I was doing everything right." And he considered himself an educated-healthy person and never missed his yearly check-ups: cardiac stress test on the treadmill or bicycle, and pharmacological stress, which uses medications to make the heart act as it would be during exercise. During this test, an electrocardiogram is taken to monitor the person's heart rate and rhythm until the exercise part is completed. It is used to show your doctor how the blood flow to your heart during exercise. It is then compared to the same images of your heart during rest. There are various methods of stress testing, and all of his tests were negative. However, he was about thirty pounds overweight, but he had recently started on a low carbohydrate diet and lost 10 pounds. His career as a welder/mechanic was stressful, hard work.

Suddenly, a very strange feeling came over him and it was so severe that he had to sit down and catch his breath and have something to eat. Afterwards, he felt better and was able to go back to work. He called and told Danielle what had happened at work. She felt, as a cardiac registered nurse, that she needed to pump his brain for the signs and symptoms of possible cardiac problems.

Signs and Symptoms of a heart attack:

Weakness
Sweating
Chest pain
Shortness of breath
Shoulder pain
Numbness or tingling in the arms
Jaw pains

Finally, Napoleon said, "I know what you are thinking. I can assure you that this is not something a Tylenol or aspirin is going to cure."

When he came home, he called up each of their children and told them what was going on and he said he thought it was very serious. He felt like he had a blocked artery in his legs and the blood was not getting to his heart like it was supposed to.

Danielle felt he was right and that now, they needed to know for sure what to do. She called Dr. Scott Eisenberg, a brilliant cardiologist with a wonderful bedside manner. He has a caring tone voice when he speaks to his patients. He listens to them with a caring attitude. He came highly recommended. He is Danielle's family cardiac doctor and she would trust him with her life. She knew he would do everything possible to find and fix the problem.

She called his office in a panicked voice, to tell him that her husband was having problems and he felt that he had blocked arteries. He could feel that his blood sugar was dropping and he felt faint. His father was also a diabetic and other doctors had told him that his blood sugar ran on the low side at times. Napoleon took the day off and went for a glucose tolerance test (GTT). He arrived at Dr. Eisenberg's office right after he completed his GTT.

Danielle felt that her husband would be able to relax after he knew for sure what was going on. The doctor ordered a blood test to measures his levels of C-reactive protein (CRP), homocysteine LDH and HDL. Homocysteine is an independent risk factor for heart disease. If present in high levels, homocysteine is linked to significantly higher risk for both heart disease and vascular disease. Then Dr. Eisenberg told Napoleon to come back on Monday for a cardiac catheterization, just to make sure he had not overlooked anything.

Danielle felt good about the test and they were anxious about the cardiac catheter, knowing they would feel better when it was behind them. She knew that she would trust Dr. Eisenberg's decision one hundred per cent.

She made dinner early that morning before they left to go to the hospital because Napoleon kept telling Danielle that he was hungry and he could not wait to come back home to eat his dinner. Napoleon told her that he was not afraid of having the catheterization done, and he felt he had the best doctor for the job.

He called the children the night before and told them not to worry; he would be all right. Danielle felt he was preparing them for the worst yet to come. She felt that he knew he was going to have long and trying days ahead of him. Danielle was never worried. She felt deep down inside that he was going to be all right and she didn't want the kids to worry about him. She remembers saying to him, "Napoleon, I know what you are thinking, but I have news for you. You are not going to die." She told him that it was possible that he had some blocked arteries, but he wouldn't be the first to have open-heart surgery and he wouldn't be the last one. She told him that God was not finished with him yet and he would have many goodbyes without saying "I think I am going to die."

He called Melissa up that night first and told her not to worry; he was going to be all right, but that he might has to have heart surgery. He told her he loved her as if he was saying his last goodbye. Danielle felt his pain, and was reading in-between the lines. Napoleon waited up so he could call JR. and he told him the same thing, as if he had a tape recorder inside his brain. Their son is studying to become a doctor. He is a very knowledgeable individual and he felt his pain when he heard that his father was ill.

Napoleon hung up the phone and said, "Now I fell better, after speaking with the children". Danielle felt that Napoleon was saying his last goodbye daddy talk. After he hung up the phone, Danielle told him that she understood what he was doing, but she had news for him. "Napoleon, you are not going to die and leave me here". You are not the first one to have this cardiac catheter done and if you need open-heart surgery, Danielle will make sure she will get the best doctor money can buy, so do not even think that you are going to die. She have hope and faith in God. You know, Napoleon, God is not ready for you yet!! This is just a test of your faith. Napoleon, please be careful the way you handle this one.

Things work in mysterious ways. There may be some hard times ahead of us. We will make it if you just hold on and be strong. Look at you father he lived to be 90 years old. God will give you strength when you feel like slipping away."

Danielle believed that when things went wrong like they sometimes do, God was trying to mold us in the way he needed us to be. God sometimes brings the sweetest blessings through the situations we shun most, the failures we fear most, or the people we avoid most.

On Monday, January 20, 2003

apoleon checked himself into a near by Community Medical Center. He wanted to get to the bottom of this problem once and for all. He were one of Dr. Scott Eisenberg second case. He were unable to eat anything after twelve midnight the night before. He were allied to take only his blood pressures medications with a sip of water that morning.

Napoleon had me to make dinner before we left for the hospital. Danielle made his favor foods cabbages bake sweet potatoes, and bake chicken breasts. We were planning to have a peaceful and relaxing eve after his cardiac catheterization. Before the test it is very important for the physician to check the patient, for allergy to iodine, shellfish . For the appropriate measures, to be carried out.

A cardiac catheterization usually doesn't require general anesthesia. Napoleon requested to have a mild anesthetic. But he was drift on and off to sleep. A dye is injected into his heart arteries through a slender catheter inserted into his right groin large femoral artery. A guided through the arteries to the heart using a moving x-ray image on film and then an angiogram is made of Napoleon heart in full. It is used to determine coronary artery blockages. Napoleon has left main disease's and his only hope to survive is open-heart surgery. Napoleon can not image his worsted night mare was now becoming a reality and it would change his life forever. Danielle stood waiting and praying in the corridor area for Dr. Eisenberg to blast through those doors any minute now. Her imagination was running away with her.

Melissa had asked Danielle if she wanted her to come home and wait with her, and Danielle told her she would be all right and she would call her the minute the procedure completed.

Danielle felt that there was no point for Melissa to come home. She heard this little voice deep down inside of her telling her that he was in trouble and she could hear her husband's voice telling her that he was right; he knew he had a blockage. Danielle still have flashbacks about the way she felt when she had a pulmonary embolism. She felt that God wanted Napoleon to be strong and prepare the children for what to expect further down the road. Napoleon was trying to say goodbye to the children, without saying it. Danielle was listen to what he was not saying to them. Danielle knew deep down inside that he was going to be all right, no matter what, and she was ready for it. Danielle felt she was just going to put her seatbelt on and wait for this fast ride. Danielle felt what ever happen they would face it together. Danielle looked at this problem as if it was a red rose bud unfolding, and she be taken Napoleon back home soon.

She knew that within the next few minutes, they would both know for sure what the problem was and not have to speculate anymore.

Danielle walked back and forth on the outside of the cardiac lab department, waiting and praying. "God, let me remember that life is full of surprises." She felt that she had to recognize and acknowledge her helplessness, before she could move on. Danielle remembers when she was growing up she read in the Bible; "Those who wait for the Lord shell renew their strength, they shall mount up with wings like eagles, they shall run and not be weary, they shall walk and not faint". At that moment Danielle realized something that she was relied solely on the doctor's and forgetting the power of God. Danielle began to pray to God for giving Napoleon a doctor with his skills and medical knowledge, compassionate and caring heart. Danielle did not stop to see *"God outstretched hands nor did she hear God saying I am here for you"* Danielle felt like she was loosing it waiting for the answers, and God had been there all along, waiting for her to just lean on him. It was at that moment she felt that positive energy and recognizes as essential to pray. Danielle let God know that He was helping simply by being there. She received strength, courage, faith and she put her trust in Him and the doctor. Danielle felt deep, deep down inside of Napoleon his determination and toughness and she knew her husband would survive. She felt that God had given her husband the energy to survive. She knew that there were times when life battered and bruised us and tried to knock us down, but Danielle would not let it succeed, she fought back when she was critical ill with the strength from her husband telling her to hang in there. She felt that now it her tern to tell her husband to hang in there and together we both stand. Danielle gritted her teeth and smiled right into life's face. She felt that this was another test and that *"this too shall pass."* She would not blame God. She would not curse him. Danielle felt that God would not deny her. "God, you created me to cry. God, you created me to laugh and rejoice." Danielle knew that God would never abandon her. God had been a father to her when she became fatherless; a mother to her when she became motherless. She could feel his presence right beside her. She could feel the Angels all around her; an echo of voices telling her to be strong and they would keep her from falling. This, too, was just another test and God would not leave her. Danielle felt His presence as she looked to her left and looked to the right. She heard a little voice inside her saying, "I am one step away. Just you be strong."

All of a sudden, those brown double doors swung wide open. Dr. Scott Eisenberg was walking through and she knew from the frown on his face, and the shaking of his head that it was not good news, and the time had come when what she dreaded the most was now a reality. As the doctor was talking and telling her about the results of the cardiac catheter, Danielle felt like he was talking about someone else. She felt very lost. She felt that with a blink of an eye, she was spellbound. Dr. Scott Eisenberg tried to reassure her that everything was going to be all right.

Danielle could not think straight at the moment; she was in state of shock. She knew that what she had dreaded all along was now a reality. Within zero seconds, her world had come tumbling down right before her eyes. Things would never be the same again.

She felt her mind go blank as if she were having a senior moment. Danielle felt like this empty shell just standing there. She heard the doctor's voice, echoing. What in the world he talking about? He can not be talking about her husband; Deep down inside of her, she felt so lost and all alone, stuck out in the wilderness. She felt like she had lost her mind, and it was not her at all. Danielle tried to speak, but the words would not come of her mouth. The doctor hugged her, turned, and walked away.

Danielle just stood there staring out the window, trying to pull herself back together. Then she heard this soft voice calling her name. She slowly turned around and it was one of her angels, Richeem she gave Danielle a hug and as they were walking away, she told Danielle that she was sent to her by one of her guardian angels, Mrs. Valentine. She just wanted to make sure you were all right. Richeem wanted to know what she could do for her. Danielle looked at her with her sad face and watery eyes and said I love you, thank you for coming. "Danielle I just has to call my daughter".

Danielle tried to call her several times, but was unable to remember Melissa's phone number. She felt like she had a blockage in her head. Danielle told Richeem that she wanted to see her husband. As she walked into the recovery room, they were rolling him back to his room on a stretcher- bed. The very first words out of his mouth were, "How did I do on the test?"

Danielle told him the test was over, but that she did have some good news and some not so good news!! "You were right. It is very serious." Napoleon said what wrong?, but as she started to tell him, his doctor walked into the room and he sat down and explained in detail about Napoleon's cardiac catheter.

Dr. Scott Eisenberg sat down in a chair alongside of his bed. He told Napoleon that he had some good news and some not so good news. He said, "You have left main disease, meaning that ninety percent of your left main artery is blocked. The left main coronary artery divides into the left anterior descending and the circumflex arteries, and the left main coronary artery supplies about two-thirds of the muscle with blood and is a very important blood vessel. The good news is that I found it in time, so we can fix it by doing open-heart surgery. What the surgeon will do is replace with a length of vein taken from your leg or with part of a mammy artery from under your ribs and bypass the blockage. The surgeon will by-pass the blockages and use tiny stitches to put the arteries back together and then the blood can circulate back to the heart in a normal cycle. But don't worry you will be all right and you will be home within five days or so. If you have the surgery on Friday, then by Sunday, you will be out of bed watching the Super Bowl game in your room."

Her husband took a long look at the doctor as if he was saying, "Are you crazy?"

As he was leaving the room, Dr. Eisenberg told Napoleon that if he needed anything day or night, have the nurses call him. He shook Napoleon's hand, gave Danielle a hug goodbye, and left the room. Napoleon looked up at her with those tiger-color eyes and he noticed that she was looking sad. He gave her a tight hug and told her that big daddy was going to be all right.

Danielle told him she was going to speak with the children and let them know the results of his cardiac catheterization.

Danielle had talked with Melissa early that day and she was telling her something about a physician on one of those Famous Talk Show's. And there was this one out standing doctor by the name of Dr. Mehmet C. Oz, M.D. he suppose to be the best Cardiothoracic Surgery in the country. But he only work in New York City, Melissa will let me know more about him tomorrow. "Napoleon I know you will take good care of me" "And you will do the right thing"

Danielle told him she was going to speak with the children and let them know the results of his test.

Danielle followed the transportation person as they took Napoleon to his room where he would stay for the next few days until he had his surgery. Napoleon's friends and family made sure he would be going to the best room in the house on the 10th floor with an ocean view, red wall-to-wall carpet and even a built-in large TV screen.

Danielle felt that his Angels were looking out for him, since he had the best room on the floor. When they arrived on the floor, all the nurses were eager to take care of him and that made her feel at ease, leaving him in the best of hands with the best warm and caring nurses, from the top down.

Danielle felt she had to make sure everything went well, because Napoleon had put his life in her hands. She helped settle him in and gave him a kiss on his cheek. He told her to go home and take care of their dog, Dexter, who was waiting for her to come home and feed him.

She arrived home in about ten minutes. She sat in the chair and the tears started to roll down her cheeks. Her dog came over to her, trying to comfort her with a kiss and he laid his head on her lap. He was whining and had tears in his eyes, as if he was trying to tell her not to worry. Napoleon was going to be all right and he would be back home soon.

Danielle felt she had to pull herself together and she called her daughter and son so they could decide what was best for their father.

As a family, they decided that night what would be the best thing to do for their father and for her husband. Melissa had done some research and found out about the doctor, who was on the famous talk show talking about doing open-heart surgery, and how he had taken on the most difficult cases and they walked out of the hospital in five days feeling great.

Melissa told Danielle that she had done her homework and found out the information they needed. Dr. Oz. worked out of the best hospital on the east coast in New York City.

Melissa called JR. and he said he would be coming home and that they should just let him know when his dad will be transferred to the New York hospital for opens -heart surgery.

Danielle said her prayers and went to bed early so that she could get up and arrive back at the hospital early the next morning. She felt an adrenal rush that she could take on the world if need be.

She suddenly felt full of energy and very alert; she would approach this problem head on.

The following morning, she rushed down the hallway and went directly to her husband's room and sat down and told him that the children and she had decided to take him to New York City for his open heart surgery and how Melissa had heard of Cardiothoracic surgeon on this famous TV talk show several times, and Danielle remembered him, too. Melissa had done research into his background. Danielle told Napoleon that the doctor's name was Dr. Oz. Danielle also called one of her cousins who also is a register nurse in the City, and she gave him an excellent recommendation. Danielle cousin Ruoshanda verified that she had heard that Dr. Oz was one of the top doctors in the country for open-heart surgery (CABG). He operated on patients who were at high risk for surgery and patients came to him from all over the world. She went on to say he is a great surgeon, he is the top of the line. He is very knowledgeable, highly skills and have a caring lovely attitude. In other words he the one for your husband surgery. Ruoshanda "If I had to have open-heart surgery I would go to him" Danielle said thank you now she can put her mind at ease.

Napoleon agreed to go and let him do the surgery, and asked that she call Dr. Scott Eisenberg. Danielle asked Dr. Eisenberg to make all the arrangements for Napoleon to go to New York City, for Dr. Oz to do the surgery.

Danielle felt so relieved after she spoke with Dr. Eisenberg who assured her that he would do whatever it takes to make things right for Napoleon. Dr. Eisenberg came and explained to us about the open- heart surgery. The doctor explained to Napoleon, "These are blood vessels that your body can do without. Some surgeons may use a combination of these grafts. When the doctor takes the vein from the leg, he will make a small incision line in the back of the knee and another at the bottom of the leg and just above the heel of the foot and you can wear shorts or swim trunks and no one will ever notice the difference. But you will have a small hairline scar in that area and your chest will have a scar in the center. Most of the scar is on the inside of the chest cavity. You will stay in the hospital about 5 days. Immediately after the surgery, you will be in the cardiac care unit for a day or two so the nurses can monitor your heart rate and rhythm and other vital signs."

Dr. Eisenberg told Napoleon he would do all of his pre-op tests that needed to be done to prepare him for the open-heart surgery, and if he needed anything or needed to talk with him about anything, he would be glad to come in and speak with him—that he should just ask the nurse to call him. He told Napoleon that the next day, he would have his Arterial Doppler study done, and a 24-hour Halter monitoring would be place on him.

After Dr. Eisenberg left the room, Napoleon looked over at Danielle and said, "I like that doctor. He explained everything very well and he talked *to* me, not just *at* me, and I felt that he really cares about me as a person, and a patient.

"All right, Napoleon," Danielle said. "I told you before that I would get you the best doctor to do the job and that someone I knew would be on your side every step of the way, and I knew he would get to the bottom of your problems and he did. I felt that the news was very shocking for all of us. But, we have to look at it from a different point of view now and be grateful that even though it is bad news, at the same time, it's good news, too, because at least they can fix the problem. There will be some long and trying days ahead of us now, but things will get better after you have the operation and you must never give up. Danielle told him she had faith in God that everything would turn out fine.

She told Napoleon that she had faith in him, too, and she would be only a second away.

Danielle told him that while he on the operating table, she would be there so that she would breathe for him when he unable to take a breath.

She said, "My heart will beat for you when they put you on the heart-lung machine and I will give you my strength to come back when your heart is placed back in your chest cavity. God will see you through this the same way He took care of me when I had the blood clot and I was home alone. God sent you to the best doctors for the job and that should tell you something.

You are the captain of the ship so stay on board and keep on pushing." Even if the tides get high rise above them and keep on pushing, until you come back to me.

Danielle felt that Dr. Scott Eisenberg was an angel sent by God in a time of need to guide them in the right direction. She felt that God was shaping and changing their world forever and things would never be the same again. She felt that God was working through them, and giving their life discomforts and challenges to test their faith in Him. And Dr. Scott Eisenberg walked in and took control and put their family at ease with the tone of his voice, had that caring attitude and facial expressions, which made things right. Dr. Eisenberg of New Jersey is a superior cardiologist. He is a bright, caring, giving doctor and he has an outstanding personality. He makes you feel like you are all part of a big, happy family.

You can call him anytime day or night and he makes you feel very special and important to him. It is not just with the patients he knows; it could be with anybody. The first thing that comes out of his mouth is, "What's wrong? What can I do for you?" I will make it right and I will do all the worrying. I just need you to be strong and hang in there."

Danielle felt that God had a plan for her husband and He had to get him prepared for the surgery by letting him go to this wedding and celebrate first, and it was not even one month later that he had to have his open heart surgery (CABG).

Danielle felt that their faith in God had planned that someone invited them to this girl's wedding on December 13, on Friday.

Napoleon was born on February 13, on a Friday, and his mother and father celebrated his birth.

And he was being invited to a wedding on December 13, on Friday, to celebrate, and one month later, he had to go into the hospital for a very serious operation.

Danielle called Lisa and she knew right away that something was wrong.

Napoleon was feeling like his old self two days later she felt it was time for her to call her friend Lisa and tell her what she been going through with her husband . She told her Napoleon is very ill and he in the hospital. He had open-heart, surgery.

On January 25, 2003, he was doing very well and Danielle said to Lisa, "Thanks to you and your daughter for saving Napoleon's life. It was no more than an act of fate and a miracle for this to have taken place.

Lisa said, "What the matter? Is it Napoleon?

Danielle said, "Yes, but he is all right now. He had to have open, heart surgery."

On January 25, she had been staying in the city to be close by Napoleon. The children had left to go back home and she and Napoleon would be in New York City until he was able to go back to Jersey.

Danielle told Lisa, "I felt you were our Angels. God had your daughter plan and set her wedding date on Friday, the 13th, and you know that we are best friends and Napoleon would not miss the wedding for anything in the world. He thinks the world of your, even more so after their father walked out on them. You know we will fill in whenever you need us. I feel that the two of you saved his life and have given our family something to celebrate, and now he has a second time around with a new life."

The doctors told him he was really and truly a miracle, walking around with only 10 percent of his left main functions. If he had passed out, he would have died and there would have been no way the medical team would have been able to bring him back.

Danielle felt there is a reason for everything that happens to us and that we need to start paying attentions and start to connect the dots. She felt that God has a way or warning us and there are times we just do not listen. We pass it off and we go around for days, weeks, months, or even years trying to figure out what went wrong. There are times it is staring you directly in the face and we just cannot see it.

Have you ever heard some folks say, "I should have done this" "or "I should have done that"? And with all of those should-haves, could-haves, and would-haves, nothing is going to change. We just blow off the smoke without the fire.

Danielle felt that Napoleon's life was plan from the day he was born.

It was a miracle God was with them throughout from the very beginning to the end. She felt that if you put your trust and faith in God, He would lead us gradually through the good times and rough times; through the valleys, storms, rain, snow, and to the sunshine.

There will be a rainbow after the rain. She felt He had sent Dr. Scott Eisenberg to do the job and lead the way for them.

Only the strong will survive

January 24, 2003

$\mathcal{N}$apoleon was transported to the best hospital in the world in New York City to have a coronary artery bypass graft (CABG) done by one of the most famous and superior Cardiothoracic surgeons in the world: Dr.Mehmet C. Oz. M.D. This doctor had appeared several times on a famous TV talk show and everyone loved him.

It was a cold and icy night and Danielle made sure her husband kept warm. He traveled with a registered nurse, a nurse's technique, the driver and herself. The nurse was an outstanding individual, with a beautiful personality. She come across as being hard and cold individual.

They arrived in New York safe and sound. It was a beautiful hospital. It had a lot of lights all over the place. If you did not know it was a hospital, you would have thought it was one of those large, fancy hotels on the strip in Las Vegas. They were greeted at the front desk and escorted to Napoleon's room. His bedroom was just breathtaking. It overlooked the river and Napoleon just loved his view. He said he felt like he was in some large resort hotel on vacation.

The registered nurses were very caring and welcomed him with open arms. The security guard informed her that she had to leave her husband's room and come back in the morning. Danielle gave her husband a kiss on his cheek and nicely left his room.

Their two children came to the hospital around 3:00 a.m. after Jr. had been driving all day to come and be with their dad.

They both met at the family home in New Jersey down by the shore. They all bunked up on the chairs in the family waiting room in the lobby for the night. There were family members of other patients sleeping all over the place down there. As Danielle looked around during the night, she felt as if they all were homeless and no one seemed to care, because they all were there for the same reason.

It was now early on Friday morning at 6:00 a.m. Danielle went to the ladies room to brush her teeth and for personal hygiene care. She felt very good and happy that within a few hours, the surgery would be over. But, she also felt that their life would be changed forever. Their life would never be the same again.

She had a change of cloths and rushed to her husband's bedside to see whether he had met his Cardiovascular surgeon, the great Dr. Oz. Napoleon told her she had just missed him. The doctor was looking forward to meeting with her to discuss his plan of care. Napoleon told her that if she rushed out to the nurses' station, he might still be there. Danielle charged out of his room down the hall to the nurses' station. As she approached the nurses' station, she recognized Dr. Oz, who was talking to two other doctors. She had seen him on one of the TV talk shows. He had this nice and caring smile when he talked. Dr. Oz looked over and saw Danielle standing there and he rushed over to introduce himself. He said, "I want to take you to my office to show you something related to your husband's surgery today." Dr. Oz told her he would be back to meet the rest of our family around 8:00 a.m. He felt she should see her husband's cardiac films first, and afterwards, he would explain everything he would be doing during the surgery. He said that Napoleon would be just like new after the surgery.

Dr. Oz took her into his office. He turned on the lights and went over to a cabinet drawer. He pulled his chart right out and it was her husband's cardiac information and he asked one of the film technicians to put it in the machine. The film started to roll and he explained everything about the surgery, and he assured her again that her husband would be better than new.

Danielle rushed back to her husband's room and told him that this doctor was some kind of a doctor. And his fingers are made out of magic , because he open the draw and out came a chart with your name on it. Danielle felt this surgeon is some kind of a godous. He was the best and she liked him. He took time with her to explain what he was going to do, but most of all, she was very impressed that he opened the drawer and pulled out Napoleon's file without looking through the drawers. She said, "He has magic hands."

Dr. Oz arrived early, walked into the room with one of his assistants and met Jr. and Melissa. Dr. Oz informed them that he would be taking care of their father. He looked over at Napoleon and told him he wanted him to be excited just like he would if his football team had won the Super Bowl game on Sunday. And he promised him he that he would be out of bed watching the game on Sunday. They all had their eyes on Napoleon and his face just lit up, and all the fear was gone. He looked so relaxed.

Dr. Oz asked Napoleon what his favorite sport? Napoleon told him football. Dr. Oz asked him, "How do you feel when your team makes a touchdown?"

Napoleon told him, "I get all excited and cheer them on." Dr. Oz said, "That's the way I want you to feel now about the surgery you are going to have in a few hours and I want you to think positive and cheer me on."

After Dr. Oz left the room, Napoleon said, " I am ready now!! Let's get on with it, and just at that moment, his brother walked into the room and they all held hands and prayed for Napoleon. Shortly after that, his gurney came for him and they all followed him down the corridor and into the pre-op holding area.

Danielle felt that her husband was going to be all right and one by one, they assured him of that. Finally, the registered nurse came and gave him his pre-op medication to help him relax. Danielle told him she would be right outside, praying for him. They all walked down the corridor to the waiting room.

Throughout the long hours, nurses kept them up-to-date on what was happening.

Danielle, thought of Dr. Oz during this surgery and she prayed for him to keep steady hands, and her thoughts turned to God and thanked Him for the gifted surgeon and for helping to guide his blessed hands. They took turns to go and have something to eat.

They must have spent more than eight hours in the waiting room designed for the families and friends of surgical patients from all over the world. The rooms were cozy, decorated in soft colors, as comfortable as waiting rooms can be. There were books, magazines, computers, and TVs, all over the place.

Danielle still can see the look on her brother-in-law's face when the registered nurse came out and informed them that they had now put Napoleon on the heart-lung machine, which maintained the flow of oxygen and blood throughout and his body while the new vessels are connected. One of his brothers turned to her and asked what that meant. Danielle tried to explain it the best she knew how. She said, "It is a machine they put patients on when they have to take the blood vessel from the chest wall and leg to bypass the blockages and restore a normal blood flow to the heart muscle for over an hour the machine is keeping his blood circulating in his body.

"You mean the machine is keeping him alive"?

"Ye, but once the surgeon repairs the heart, with the coronary artery bypass graphs to create a new source of blood for areas of the heart served by blocked arteries. However Dr. Oz , informed us the blockages in certain arteries was more then "90 percent," Napoleon was at a high risk for an heart attack. Sometimes they will stay on the heart-lung machine a little longer until they make sure his heart is all right and then they will put him on a ventilator to help him breathe in order to rest the heart for a few hours until he is fully awake. They will take the tube out and let him breathe on his own.

Napoleon is strong and he will be all right. All we can do now is pray for him and the surgeons and nurses, and everyone played an excellent roll in his surgery. Danielle felt her husband was in the best of hands and that he would be all right; she was more worried about his brothers and their two children.

Finally, Dr. Oz came out of the operating room with a big smile on his face. They all knew Napoleon was all right. He informed them that he would be just like new once he healed from the surgery and everything had gone well. He would be on a ventilator until he woke up tomorrow, which was Saturday morning. Then they would take the tube out of his mouth.

Shortly afterward, Dr. Oz came back and took them to see Napoleon in his room. He looked very weak and vulnerable under those white sheets as he lay there with the tubes hanging from his mouth. The intervenous bottles hung from the poles. His face was swollen from being under anesthesia for eight hours. Major fluid shifted in his body and altered the cardiac out-put, causing swelling. Having the respirator tube down his throat for eight hours had puffed his lips. His eyes were closed; his face pale. Danielle went to the bed, bent down, and kissed Napoleon on his forehead and softly told him he would be all right. He nodded his head. They all had tears of joy in their eyes, as they thanked God, the surgeon, nurses, and the surgical team.

Danielle had promised Napoleon she would stay close by his side until he was well enough to come back home, even if it meant sleeping on a chair or the floor in the family waiting room. His brother and the two kids did just that. In addition, there were other family members sleeping in the family waiting room.

All of the rooms for family were booked up. Even at the price of $250,00 a night. Danielle felt she would find her a room for the rest of his hospitalization. However, it had to be somewhere easy so she could be transport back and forward to the hospital each day to visit with Napoleon.

On January 25, 2003, at 5:00 a.m., Danielle awakened and rushed to her husband's bedside. He was awake and alert. She kissed him on his forehead. She looked up and silently thanked Father God for restoring life to her handsome husband.

Suddenly, she caught her breath in amazement, as the nurse's conversation reached her heart. Napolean had opened his eyes, and he recognized his wife, children and brothers. His brothers and the children said it was unbelievable; that it was great, and she heard one of his brother's say, "Thank God, and praise the Lord that he is all right." And they all had tears of joy in their eyes.

Napoleon recuperated and was discharged from the hospital in five days. He arrived out of bed early that morning after Danielle helped him get dressed for the trip back home. It was a bright and sunny cold day with snow everywhere. She put layers and layers of clothes on him. He wore a heavy brown leather coat and she wrapped a scarf around his neck and put a stocking cap on his head.

His older brother, Bruce, had driven down from Buffalo, New York, and picked Danielle and Napoleon up at the hospital and drove them back to New Jersey in one of the luxury Mercedes. It was a nice, comfortable ride for Napoleon.

Afterward, they arrived home and Danielle opened the garage door and Bruce drove the car into the garage, closed the door and assisted Napoleon out of the car. Danielle was walking up the stairs behind the two of them, as his brother was telling him to lean on him. He was his big brother and he had promised to take care of him and he was doing just that. Napoleon was 6ft. 1 inches tall, weighing around 230 pounds and he finally made it up the two flights of stairs into the bedroom.

Napoleon had tears in his eyes; he was so happy to be back home at last.

If someone asked Danielle what type of person Dr. Oz was, she would have had to say, "His smile in itself can win anyone's faith and trust. When he talks to his patient, you can see the caring in his eyes and hear it in his voice. That says it all. Dr. Oz makes eye contact as he is speaking to you and he doesn't look away or down on you. He made sure he asked if anyone has any more questions for him before his exit the room.

Napoleon felt very good about this doctor's warm and caring attitude. He made rounds to check on his patients in the morning and late afternoon and that made them feel very important. He was so nice, Danielle thought she was dreaming at times and he reminded her of Dr. Ben Casey from the TV show in the sixty's. That was one of her favorite TV shows.

Two months later, they took a Cruise on the Star Princess Ship, for ten days to warmer weather.

Cardiovascular Artery Disease

ardiac cardiovascular artery disease causes more deaths, disability and economic loss than any form of hard blood vessel (cardiovascular) disease. The condition often develops gradually and silently, typically over many years. In fact, it can go virtually unnoticed until it suddenly produces a heart attack. Approximately one million Americans have a heart attack each year. About 40 percent of these are fatal. The coronary arteries are part of your heart's own circulatory system. They provide the muscles of your heart with a steady supply of blood that carry oxygen and nutrients. The coronary arteries encircle the heart like a crown and send branches downward to the tip of the heart. When disease develops, or damage occurs in these arteries, the condition which are called (CAD), Coronary artery disease.

Danielle feels that the Aortic is that of a Mother of the four functions: the Aorta, the Aortic valve, the Mitral valve, and the left ventricle.

The Heart muscles they are oxygenated bloods from the lungs cross the mitral valve and go to the main pumping chamber of the heart.

The left ventricle

The ventricle contracts

The mitral valve close to keep the blood from leakage back into the lungs

The aortic valve opens up the gait and let the blood come into the aorta

The Aorta pick- up the blood and carries it to all parts of the body

Including the heart muscle

There are four Main coronary:

The left Main coronary artery divides into the left anterior and the circumflex arteries. The left main coronary artery about two third of the heart muscle with blood and is a very important vessel.

The right coronary artery supplies the right side and the bottom part of the heart. Blocks in this vessel can cause serious interruptions in the heart rhythm. The left anterior descending artery supplies the front wall an artery of the heart.

Blocks in this vessel can cause serious loss of strength.

The circumflex artery supplies the sidewall of the heart.

Stress Testing:

Stress testing is used to show your doctor how the blood flow to your heart looks during exercise. It is then compared to the same images of your heart during rest. There are various methods of stress testing, such as riding a bicycle or on a treadmill. Or pharmacologic stress, where medication makes the heart act as it would doing exercise. An electrocardiogram monitors your heart rate and rhythm, during, the entire exercise part of the test.

Nuclear Cardiology:

Also called diagnostic tests in which a radionuclide is injected into the blood, and a special gamma camera takes pictures of the radionuclide as it flows through your heart muscle. Nuclear tests are to evaluate the amount of blood flow delivered to the heart muscle through the coronary arteries, and measure the amount of blood pumped by the heart with each beat (called the ejection fraction).

Heart Hazards and Its Helpers

Open heart surgery(CABG) is not a cure for heart disease. It can help you only if you help yourself.

You need to make a change in your lifestyle.

Exercise: Increases the artery blood flow and strengthens the heart muscles. If you have high blood pressure, this puts a strain on your heart and damages the blood vessels.

Diet: You are what you eat, such as foods high in cholesterol or saturated fat. These foods will increase your blood cholesterol level and might block the coronary arteries.

Oxygen/Smoking

Oxygen is very important to the heart circulatory system. Smoking a cigarette of any kind will decrease the oxygen flow to the capillary blood vessels. It will cause a vascular constriction of the blood vessels and cause a temporary rise in the pressure and increase the heart rate. Sometimes you may hear a smoker say, "I stopped smoking and afterwards, I put on all this weight." Or "I smoke to stay thin. However, they need to realize that this cycle is slowly destroying their body because of a lack of oxygen.

Risk Factors of Heart Disease (CAD)

Hypertension:
High blood pressure
Obesity:
Over weight;
Homocysteine: An amino that has recently been discovered as an independent risk factor for heart disease. If present in high levels, homocysteine has also been linked to both heart disease and vascular disease. The elevated levels, of homocysteine is inexpensive and straightforward, to treat with vitamin B-complex and folic acid or take foltx 2 tables a day. It allow normal metabolism of proteins and prevent the abnormal build up of this toxic material.

Low Density Lipoprotein (LDL): is referred to as the "Bad" cholesterol, and is made in the liver. The LDL number should be less than 160, or lower depending on your other coronary risk factors.

The LDL is the major transport of cholesterol in the blood.

The overflow becomes stuck along the lining of the arteries.

High Density Lipoprotein (HDL)

The nice cholesterol HDL-35 or higher

HDL's main function is to pick up the excess cholesterol.

LDL: the tissues in the body, especially the arterial linings; they carry it back to the liver.

Lipids: they are fat and cholesterol in the blood.

A lipid analysis is a blood test and you need to fast for twelve hours.

The affects of cholesterol levels:

Your blood is affected by both what you eat and how fast your body makes and disposes of it. Cholesterol and family genes (heredity) play a role in how high your cholesterol level is by affecting how fast the LDH's are made and transported from the blood. Again, you are what you eat:

There are foods high in saturated fats. Dairy products, animal fats, also eggs yolks, and organ meats play a roll in raising the blood cholesterol level. You need to decrease the level of your intake and, therefore, you will in turn decrease your cholesterol in the blood.

However, your weight is another big factor; it will increase your LDL- cholesterol level. However, if you lose weight, it may help to lower your cholesterol in the blood.

Your physical activity also plays a role in your blood cholesterol and can help to lower the LDH- cholesterol and raise HDL-cholesterol, which is the "good" one.

Your age and gender: The blood cholesterol levels in males and females normally start to increase about at 20 years and reach it peak level about age 60; then it will level off.

In females, this will happen before menopause. Cholesterol levels are normally lower than they are for males at the same age. After menopause, it will increase to higher levels than in males.

Studies show that there is a link between high blood cholesterol and coronary heart disease.

The factors you can do something about your eating habits and your physical activity.

You need to eat a healthy diet, and keeping active is very important to keep your bad cholesterol level down. If you are unable to lower your cholesterol with diet and exercises, your doctor may prescribe medication for you.

*****

Napoleon was kept alive by the heart-lung machine for several hours so that Dr. Oz would be able to repair his heart. Napoleon also had an atrial septal defect, which is a hole in his heart. Normally, this closes up at birth. In children or young adults, this atrial septal defect is detected. The symptoms of mild fatigue, poor growth, or dyspnea on exertion may be present. If it is small, it may not need intervention, or it may close on its own. Napoleon is 6 ft.1 inches and had been very healthy up until this point. Dr. Oz promised Napoleon that he would be able to be out of bed watching the Super Bowl game on his large screen TV and he would be discharged from the hospital on the fifth day, and that he was. Napoleon, had a new slant on life. He found himself a new love and his name is Bear. Bear is with him twenty four seven, every breath he takes and with every step he makes over the course of the day. Bear held tight to his chest. Danielle's family is so grateful for the miracle, and because of God and Dr. Mehmet C. Oz, M.D., Napoleon has a second chance at life itself. God will send the right person for the job and he sent Dr. Oz. for Napoleon. Dr. Oz. were Napoleon Angel sent by God.

Napoleon said that every day when he wakes up with a heartbeat and breathing, it is another miracle in his life. His family says, "Thank You, Father God, for putting us in the right hands at the right time of this highly skilled, brilliant and highly recommended Cardiothoracic surgeon. Napoleon and his family are very grateful for having doctor Oz., for his utmost care.

Thank Dr.Mehmet C. Oz, M.D. - Cardiothoracic Surgery Director, Cardiovascular.

Still Live Beyond Those Clouds

*T*hey live on in your smile. They are always a step behind you; There are times you can feel their presence.

Danielle believes in the power of prayer; she believes in God and that He has a plan for each of us.

Danielle believes that we have a soul that will continue to live when our body is just an empty, cold hard shell.

Danielle does not believe in death. She believes we pass into a new world and we are reborn.

She believes God is within all of us and speaks to us through others folks. We should be careful how we speak or judge anyone; they could be your Angel sent from God.

Danielle believes you are never alone.

She believes in the power of God and she believes in Angels.

Danielle remembers when she was very sick and she was all alone. She prayed to God in her mind because she was as stiff and dead as dead and very cold; she was unable to move. She asked her Angels to be with her. All of a sudden, they all came and gathered at the top of her bed on her left side and at the foot of her bed and they all had sweet smells and flopping wings and there was a cool mist in the air.

Danielle was thinking to herself, what about the right side of her bed? Then as she looked way down the road, she saw this very tiny light, the size of an eye. As the light became closer, it became brighter and brighter, and out stepped God, and there were a lot of people walking behind him. It was not until she saw God that she said, "I see now why the Angels were not on the right side of my bed. They were getting ready because God was coming and they made room for Him to come on the right. God was holding His hands in a praying position.

As He slowly approached alongside of her place where she was lying on this bed, Danielle struggled to reach out her right hand just to touch His garment and she felt tears rolling down her cheeks, and at that point, she was able to move. Danielle thought about the woman in the Bible, saying that if she could touch the hem of His garment, she would know the she could hold on, and Jesus would call her Daughter.

To My Lovely Wife

What is love? It is the mystery and magic that makes the. Attraction of a man and woman, or is it a husband, lover, friend and wife?

It is falling in love with one great person for the rest of your life.

When we said, "I do", I should have known all the changes there would be.

I know I will never be the same again.

When I asked you to marry me, you told me you had to sleep on it.

And then, later on, you told me you would only be committed to five years. Now some thirty years later, we are still going strong. We are soul-mates, and no matter what, we will always be together. I just want to thank you for being my wife.

Having you for my wife makes me want to be a better man and do all that I can to please you. You make me feel like no other woman could and that makes me feel like I can do anything. You enlighten my world, body, mind, and soul.

You make my eyes glow like firework.

You lift up my spirit and I will never forget the first time you and my nurse got me up after my open heart surgery.

You said, "Stand tall and walk like a soldier." I took one look at your serious face. I knew you were not playing and that showed me how much you cared for me.

I knew you had my best interest at heart.

You were there cheering and encouraging me to stand tall and march like a soldier and hold on to your brown bear. I will forever be grateful for you and the love you showed me.

In the good times and the bad, somehow we got through.

Somehow, I continue to keep falling in love with you and each day I love you more and more. I am so glad I found you and you felt something for me, and it was enough for you to marry me and call me your husband.

Thank you for your love.

Forever, Yours

Vision of Fate

$\mathcal{T}$imes change; people's lives change forever within a flash. It is a brilliant sunny morning, and a gently soothing breeze is coming from the Atlantic Ocean. The sky is baby blue in color, with no clouds in sight, on 09/11/2001.

Danielle was looking forward to going to the city and she felt good about herself. She got out of bed early and saw her husband off to work. He kissed her on the cheek and told her to have a nice time in the city and he wished he was going with her, but somebody had to go to work.

As Danielle got dressed for the city, she was thinking what a nice day she would have before she had to meet with her acting producer. However, her appointment was not until 3:00 p.m. She had tried to change it several times, but was unable to. For the life of her, she could not understand why she had to wait until 3:00pm today.

Finally, Danielle said, "All right, I will leave New Jersey at 10:00 a.m. instead of 7:00 a.m. and she would arrive at 11:00 a.m. instead of 8:00 a.m. Danielle decided that she would go to the supermarket to pick up a few items for dinner, before she go to the City today.

Danielle had talked with her daughter on Sunday night in Boston, and she was in somewhat of a hurry about going on

a business trip to Florida on Monday morning. Danielle assured her daughter she would be all right, but deep inside, a little voice.

They continued to tell her that something was going to happen, but Danielle could not put her finger on it

She refused to accept that idea; instead, she prayed for her daughter to have a safe flight. Her daughter had been flying all over the world. The whole time, Danielle felt an intuition that frightened her, but she did not want to frighten her daughter. Danielle kept trying to push it out of her consciousness. She had strong vive about the airplane, but she could not put her finger on it. She felt like her mind was playing tricks on her.

Her daughter called her after she arrived and informed Danielle that she had arrived all right and she was on her way to take care of business. Danielle told her joking around that she thought she would be hi-jacked to Cuba.

Danielle felt a need to call the studio and speak to her director about coming to the city and trying out for a part in an up- coming show. She said she would like an appointment for 9:00 a.m. if at all possible, because she could be there early if that was okay with him. He told her that he would check and see if he had any openings at that time. He came back to the phone and told her that he had a very important meeting at 9: 00 a.m. Nevertheless, he would call her if he could fit her in before the meeting.

Danielle had received a postcard, telling her that her appointment was for September 11, 2001, at 3:00 p.m. She felt that he had made a mistake on September 10. She called the studio and asked him to clarify her time because she thought there was a mistake. Danielle waited a few seconds so he could check the time. He came back and told her to please come around 3:00 p.m. She told him she would greatly appreciate it if she could see him in the morning at 8:00 a.m. He asked her to hold on again and he came back and told her that he was sorry, but he had just booked someone else for that time.

Danielle hung up the phone and she felt she would just take the 10:00 a.m. bus and would arrive in the city by 11:15 a.m. Then she would just go downtown, have some lunch and go shopping. Danielle felt she had to arrive early that day so she could get herself together. Her husband kissed her on the cheek and told her to be careful and have a good day in the city. He wished he could go with her, but someone had to go to work. Then he smiled and walked away. She put her dog outside and fed him his breakfast and the she decided to run to the store for a few items for dinner.

As she walked inside of her house, Danielle heard the phone ringing. At first, she just started to let it ring and then she heard her husband yelling at the top of his voice, telling her not to go to New York. " Don't go to New York?" she asked him. "What's wrong with you? Are you going crazy?" She said she would wait and go at 12:00, noon because her appointment was not until 3:00p.m., and things would be calm down by that time.

Napoleon said, "Don't go to New York today at all. Turn on the TV. And you will see what I am talking about. A plane has hit the T win Towers." From the tone of his voice, he was very upset. Danielle turned the TV, it was terrifying, and to see all of those people is jumping out of the windows.

Napoleon called the kids to make sure they were all right. "You know Melissa is in Florida on a business trip. She will call JR. and make sure he is okay." Danielle was shaking so badly that she dropped the phone. She began to cry so hard and she could not understand what was happen in the City. She had no ideal what was going on. Danielle felt she had to speak with her son. She picked up the phone and began to dial his number. Finally, she was able to reach him. JR. are you all right? Yes Mom. JR told his Mom that he was supposed to be downtown in New York for three days this week, doing a commercial. At the last minute, he decided to call the camera group Friday and changed it until the following week.

Danielle did not know that her son was supposed to be in the City this week. She felt it was fate and God had saved all of their lives. The three of them had escaped death. She felt happy and guilty at the same time. Tears rolled down her face by the bucketfuls and she dropped to her knees thanking God for taking care of her children and keeping them safe.

She hung up the phone and as she was watching the news, she got down on her knees and began to pray for the American people and none American. She felt that this country would never be the same again. Danielle felt their pain and frustration, loss, dying and their poor families' grief. She prayed for their faith of the inner soul, and that they might find peace within. Her strength and courage come from God. Deep, deep within her, implanted by his very hands is her faith, hope and determination.

Her fate and will to survive
Hug yourself tight
Tell yourself you love you.
Tell your wife or husband you love him or her.
Tell your family and friends you love them.
Never put off today for tomorrow what you want to do today.

Danielle felt that God had blocked their path to protect them in time of trouble. Now she could see how God worked to protect her from danger. She felt so nauseous and angry at herself.

Faith will give you strength and a vision, and faith will guide you if you stand still.

Danielle felt that rushing makes waste and time is a venture.

We must pay attention to what someone is telling us. They just might save your life. They might shield you when there is no way out. Danielle also felt that faith had brought her peace in the midst of the storms.

That inner peace of self will make the world a better place

Tell your children they are special and a gift from God.

His love is unconditional.

Danielle felt for the first time in the history of American that we was treated equal and we felt each other pain

We see no color, nor rich or poor. We are all one large family.

We are all trying to stay out of harms way.

We are glad to be Americans.

Danielle felt this, too, would pass.

In addition, all of those lives that had crossed over were not in vain. We all have learned something, as she and her family love, faith, hope and God and Angels was watching over our family.

We thank you father God-----Peace

I've Been There Before

Hawaii

anielle felt that she had a need to travel around the world to visit different places, and talk with people of all walks of lives.

One of her hot spots is Hawaii; it is here that brings out the best in her.

She feels that it is nature – maybe the smelling of the dampness after a rainfall.

Or it could be the mist in the air or the waterfalls, or maybe when she inhales fresh air.

There is the smell of fresh waterfalls.

The shapes and sizes of the mountains and those

Hawaiian flowers, green tress. Could it be because the bodies itself are made up of tiny small cells and they are all floating around in the water?

Danielle felt that whatever the body needs, the message will be sent to the brain.

She grew up in Alabama near the river and as children. So she liked the wildlife. They had their own man made ponds and underground spring water.

They would call it "Good Old Water" when they were kids.

Danielle has a love for water, and the sound of the water, crashing against the rocks is very relaxing. It is here at the ocean that she can sit down, forget about her troubles, and let the water wash them out into the deep blue sea.

She feels that the water is a cleansing sensation throughout her body and very soul. It is such a marvelous and beautiful feeling. It makes her feel a need to become aware of her soul and spirit. It helps her to see clearly and feel alive.

What's wrong with this Man?

After 35 years, he still wants to remarry Danielle?!!
She said she told him five years and now it was over 30 years! She was shocked to see him down here and so was the minister.

This picture was taken in a small church in Las Vegas, Nevada.

"Why not?" she asked.

"I cannot stand for you to beg," she said. "I think you are so funny. I will divorce you on Monday morning. Okay? Ha, Ha,"

Hello World

Do Things you love.

Have Fun.

Time out

There is nothing Melissa cannot do!!

She can fly.

Oh, my child what is a mother to do-do???

"I told you I was an Angel, didn't I?"

My Son & his dog
Max,

Hey, Dude "It hot out here"

That water looks GOOD.

I can taste it.

Hey Man how bout-- a Swim-m?

Zap, Tap, Zip

Daddy, say What Man?

Hey Dad

Take me, Man.

Hurry up. I am busy too. You want me to stand up here all day?

Che-ee-se

How you like that?

Pop!

Dexter Dog

Hey- Man

I will trunk-it

today.

The Nurse's Guide

Guide her cheeks that she may keep a smile on her face
Guide her hands, Lord, while she care for her patient's
Guide her brain, Lord, while she count all of those medications
Guide her vision that she may see beyond the end of her shift
Guide her ears that she may hear every single call-light that rings.
Guide her knowledge that she be able to teach her patients.
Guide her spirit that she enlighten every patient she touch today
Guide her talents that she makes just one person laugh and forget about there problems for just a little while
Guide her feet that she may roll skate down that long corridor.
Guide her feeling that she may approach the patient bedside with a caring and understanding attitude.
Guide her strength that she might feel strong by the end of the day.
God, thank for your Guide today.

The Right Moment

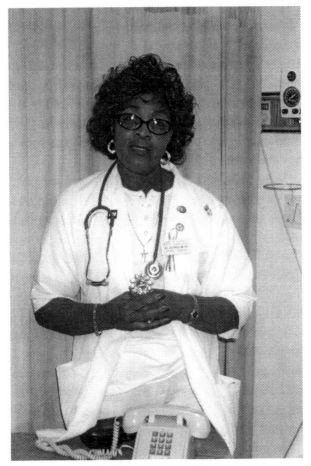

nurse holding the hem of the garment

ometimes things happen for a reason
While chatting with one of her patients about her faith
In God, and how he saved her life after she touched the hem of his
garment, a priest was at her bedside and he said, "You are not going
to believe this, but I have a piece of his garment in my pocket."

She was in a state of shock, and on that day, she had her camera
in her locker.

To Love, To Be Loved

To have and to hold and have you ever gazed at the stars in the sky and asked yourself,

"Why am I here?"

or, what is my purpose here in the grand scheme of things?

One incredible gift has come out of Danielle's quest to know God. She has discovered the " Biggest Picture" of her life. She now sees the stars in the sky as guiding lights of clarity as she awakens to her reason for waking up to inspire by her soul and to inspire others by telling her story from her soul.

Her life like yours, has been full of ups and downs, twists and turns. She never dreamed she would be lucky enough to find a real man like Napoleon who lifted her up above everything else that came her way.

Her life is rich and full. It is not because of what she is doing, but rather, how she is as a wife, and mother. She sees her children as true gifts from God. They show her the love that she has – a partner with whom she shares a conscious relationship.

They have come together to love and to hold, and to remind each other of God's love.

Danielle feels that our purpose in life is to inspire and to be inspired, and life has become the blossoming of the fruit on the vine. She is discovering who she is, and what is possible in her world as she lives from a place of acceptance and love.

Color Is Not Important

Color is not important to me;

What I do each day is.

I help people in all lifestyles;

I will take away your pain.

Yelling, "Oh, God, please help me;

I cannot take this pain."

"I lay here on this stretcher bleeding from head to toe;

I dare not to care."

Color is not important to me; your care is.

There's hope in those eyes. There is a cry or pain in your voice.

I here doctors yelling "oxygen, needle, thread, dressing, packing,

please."

Color is not important to me; your care is.

I hear another doctor yelling "Give oxygen, stat lasix, I/V push,

stat 1mg morphine I/V push, stat Ekg (electrocardiogram), stat

ABG's (Arterial blood gases) stat chest x-ray, state blood work,

now today."

The noise is hearted – heavy, loud, crying, and moaning:

"God help me, help me!

Not a minute later;

No word spoken;

No heartbeat heard;

No pulse felt;

No worry in this old world

Color is not important to me; your care is.

The Angel Next Door

There was this woman in a very serious car accident and did not expect to recover. She came across this male nurse who cared for her day in and day out. Needless to say, he fell madly in love with her at first site. She did not share those same feelings for him and after several months of dating each other, they broke up and went their separate ways. However, she was pregnant with his baby and she never told him about she was expecting a baby. When the baby was born, she gave it up for an adoption. And she moved on with her life as if nothing never happen.

Some twenty years later, there were this little boy adopted by these very rich people, who already had two little girls and they just wanted a boy to make their life complete. They applied to an adoption agency, and a few days later, they received a phone call. "Mrs. Collins, we have a nice baby boy. He is just a few days old. We'd like to know how soon you can come pick the baby up."

Mrs. Collins told them as soon as she could contact her husband, who was presently at his office. They both were very excited about this little baby boy, and their little girls were happy to have a baby brother and they were all one big happy family.

All down through life, the little boy felt as if he did not fit in. He felt he was adopted. One day, he approached his parents and they informed him that he was right, but they loved him as if he were there own biological child. The young man knew deep down inside that he felt his life would never be complete until he knew who his real parents were.

Over thirty years later, he fell in love and married on August 16, 1999. He had two boys of his own. This young man set out to search for his biological family. He loved his adopted parents and they were good to him and made sure he had everything he needed. But one thing was missing and that was the love that comes from your real mother and father. He felt that his adoptive parents loved him, but it was not like the love they showed their own two girls and that bothered him. More than thirty year later, in searching for his parents, he found out that he lived a few doors down from his real father and never knew it. He finally located his real mother and found out where he was born and she told him his father's name on his birth certificate.

He learned later that the name on his birth records was not his real name; the last name was real, but not the first, so this confused him more. One day, he was doing some work at another man's house who lived down the street from him and he began to question this man about the man he had been searching for, for over thirty years. The man said, "You can ask him yourself."

He was shocked when the man walked out of the room. He looked just like him, and he knew that this was his real dad. He finally met his real sister and they found out they both were married on the same day August 16, 1999, three years apart, and they both have two little boys and they named their firstborn the same name, Robert.

Just when you feel things cannot get any worse, unfortunately, they can. His real dad, George, had a very close friend who was slowly wasting away and he felt for months that his life would stand still the day she crossed over. God sent someone to fill the empty space in his heart – a son, two lovely grandchildren, and a lovely daughter-in-law.

He, himself, is fighting cancer; his girlfriend is dying from some deadly disease which has no cure and he just completed his chemotherapy. The doctors told him he in excellent health and a few months later, he ended up in the hospital for a permanent pacemaker.

Danielle feels that when a person thinks that their life is a roller coaster and they are unable to get off, they should exhale, look around and you will see someone who has it far worse than you. Danielle believes that when one door closes, another one will open. God said He would take care of you.

Call A Codes

Call a Code Stat.

I'll be bouncing all over your chest; there is no pulse.

All clear, you are clear; I am clear.

Shock, Shock, Shock

No pulse bouncing rock, bouncing rock

Normal saline wide open, epinephine 1mg I/V push atropine 1 mg I/V.

No, not another patient has died and left me to fend for her.

I did not know her name, yet after she crossed over, I felt her pain.

Color is not important to me; her care is.

Why do I feel this way?

Why do I do this? I will never know. Another one has passed into another new world.

Until the next person in pain comes rushing through those doors, chest pain, shortness of breath, strokes, full of blood, legs, arms, eyes, fingers, nose, gunshots wounds, traumas.

Bones broken and hanging off. nurse's job is never done. When the codes are over, the prayers have just begun.

Pulmonary Embolism

efinition: pulmonary embolism is an obstruction of one or more pulmonary arteries by a thrombus it originating somewhere in the venous system or in the right side of the heart. A flowing clot is known as an embolus. An embolus travels from the systemic venous circulation through the right side of the heart and into the pulmonary arterial system. Once it reaches a branch to small for it to pass through , and it becomes impacted, obstructing the flow of blood in that vessel. Pulmonary embolism is an extremely common and highly lethal condition that is a leading cause of death in all age groups.

According to the American Heart Association, an estimated 600,000 people develop

Americans develop pulmonary embolism annually and there are 60,000. Die from it each year.

In the US: PE is the third most common cause of death in the US, with at lease 650,000 cases occurring annually. It is the first or second most common cause of unexpected death in most age groups. The highest incidence of recognize PE occurs in hospitalized patients. Autopsy results show that as many as 60% of patients dying in the hospital had a PE, but the diagnosis has been missed in about 70% of the cases. Surgical patients has long been recognized to be at special risk for deep vein thrombosis (DVT) and PE, but the problem is not confined to surgical patients, studies show that acute DVT may be demonstrated in as of the following.

Medical patients placed on bed rest for a week 10-13%

Patients in medical intensive care unit 29-33%

Pulmonary disease kept in bed for 3 or more days 20-26%

Patients who are asymptomatic after coronary artery bypass graph 48%

As many as 25,000 Americans are hospitalizes each year for pulmonary emboli, they are relatively common complication in hospitalized patients.

Even without warning signs and symptoms pulmonary embolism can cause sudden death.

Pulmonary embolism caused by large clots can cause sudden death, usually within 30 minutes of when symptoms began.

Etiology: Risk Factors:

For thrombus formation Stasis of venous circulation, in the blood vessels with injury to the endothelial lining-leads to intravascular clotting, A thrombus, fat or tumor; tissue, air amniotic fluids.

More than 90% of the cases of pulmonary embolism are complications of stoke, postoperative state, obesity, diabetes mellitus, hypercoagulability of the blood; History of thromboembolism

A high concentration of estrogen, sickle cell anemia, pregnancy, polycythemia vera, thrombocytopenia, sepsis, trauma, aging inflammatory process, prolong bed rest, immobilization, cancer, heart attack, heart surgery, congestive heart failure, fractures of the hips or femur.

Pathophysiology:

More than 90% of thrombi develop in the deep veins of the lower extremities.

Thrombus formation enhances platelet adhesiveness and causes release of serotonin and there is vasoconstrictor of the bronchial passages, decreasing lung volume and compliance.

The clot moves to pulmonary vessels, where it stop a in the first vessel it is too large to move through. The ventilation continues, but perfusion is decreased, leading to ventilation perfusion mismatch of the venous blood. The alveolar collapse and atelectasis develop because the alveoli cannot produce enough surfactant to maintain alveolar integrity; these factors increase pulmonary artery pressure and intrapulmonary shunting.

The pulmonary embolism is one of the most common acute respiratory disorders in hospitalized patients.

Morality/Morbidity:

Massive: more then 50% occlusion of pulmonary blood flow; caused by occlusion of a lobar artery or larger artery.

Submissive: less than 50% occlusion of pulmonary blood flow PE is one of the most common causes of unexpected death, being second to coronary artery disease as a cause of sudden unexpected natural death at any age.

Most clinicians do not appreciate the extent of the problem, because the diagnosis is unsuspected until autopsy is approximately 80% of cases.

PE often is fatal, prompt diagnosis and treatment can reduce the mortality rate dramatically.

Approximately 10% of patients in whom acute PE is diagnosis die within the first 10 minutes

The diagnosis of PE missed more than 400,000 times in the US each year, and approximately patients die who would have survived with the right diagnosis and treatment.

History: PE is so common and so lethal the diagnosis they are serious in every patient who presents with any chest symptoms that we are unable to figure out.

Symptoms:

chest pain, chest wall tenderness, back pain, shoulder pain, upper abdominal pain, syncope, Hemoptysis, shortness of breath, painful respiration, new onset of wheezing, any new cardiac arrhythmia, or Shortness of breathe that may occur suddenly.

Sudden, sharp chest pain that become worse with deep breathing or coughing, wheezing

Sweating, fainting (syncope)

Anxiety coughing up blood,

Fainting, Heart palpations

Chest pain: under the breastbone or on one side

Sharp stabbing or burning, aching, dull, and heavy sensation

may be worsened by breathing deeply, coughing, eating, bending, and stooping. Other symptoms: are a suspicion of PE must include chest pain, chest tenderness, back pain, shoulder pain, upper abdominal pain, syncope, hemoptysis, shortness of breath, painful respiration, also new onset of wheezing, any new cardiac problems, sudden onset of dyspnea

Pleuritic chest pain,

Apprehension, restlessness, feeling of impending doom, dry cough, hemoptysis, and tachycardia.

Distend neck veins, cyanosis, S3 or S4 heart sound

Positive Homans' sign, Syncope

Low arterial carbon dioxide partial pressure value

Petechiae over chest, diaphoresis

Other symptoms her associated with this disease:

Wheezing, skin, skin discoloration, bluish

Nasal flaring, low-grade fever, pelvis pain, leg pain in one or both legs, swelling in the legs in lower extremities

Lump associated with a vein near the surface call the superficial vein, may be painful, low blood pressure

Pulses weak or absent, light headness, fainting spells, sweating, anxiety, positive Homans' sign

Danielle felt a little tapping: She awaken by tapping on the foot of her bed. It jumped on her legs and paralyzed her entire body.

She felt this fuzzing kissing her face.

She felt heavy pressure on her chest.

She felt severe chest pain, difficulty

Breathing and feeling of impending doom

Diagnosis:

Pulmomary embolism can be diagnosis through the patient history, a physical examination, and diagnostic tests including chest x- may be normal.

Arterial blood gas measurements; hypoxemia and acid –base imbalances, and leg vein ultrasonography or venography and a spiral scan.

Electrocardiogram (ECG); right axis deviation, tall peaked T waves, ST segment changes, and T-wave inversion in V1- V4 leads

V/Q scan; ventilation/perfusion mismatch (interruption of blood flow to affected lung area)

Pulmonary angiography (the definitive test but invasive); location and extent of embolus

Pulmomary Embolism Management

To restore normal tissue perfusion and decrease the risk of further obstruction, pulse oximetry; administer oxygen therapy to correct hypoxia. Obtain artery blood gases (ABG) Intubation and mechanical ventilation for severe hypoxemia;

Anticoagulation with intravenous heparin (bolus followed by continuous infusion) during the acute phase;

Warfarin (Coumadin). Coumadin is an anticoagulant. Anti means against, and coagulant refers to blood clotting. An anticoagulant help reduce clots from forming in the blood. Orally when the heparin drip is discontinued, with prothrombin time and partial thromboplastin time monitored closely; Administer, oral anticoagulants concomitantly with heparin for 3 to 4 days before switching to orally agents alone therapy is continued until the international normalized ratio (INR) is 2.0 to 3.0;

Administer steroids to decrease local injury to tissue and to decrease pulmonary edema if the source is a fat embolus.

Coumadin; blocks the formation of vitamin K-dependent clotting factors in your liver. Vitamin K is needed to make clotting factors that help the blood to clot and prevent bleeding. Vitamin K is also, found in naturally foods such as leafy, green vegetables and certain vegetable oils.

Coumadin reduces the body's ability to make blood clots. It can help stop harmful clots from getting larger. Coumadin does not break up existing blood clots.

Coumadin generally begins to reduce blood clotting within 24 hours after taking the drug.

The full effect make take 72 to 96 hours to occur. The anti-clotting effects of a single dose of coumadin last 2 to 5 day. However, it is important for you to take you dose as prescribed by you doctor or healthcare provider.

Monitor coagulation studies (partial thromboplastin time for heparin and prothrombin time oral agents) to maintain levels at 1 ½ to 2 times normal values.

Close monitoring to protect the patients from situations that could lead to bleeding.

Surgical interventions: Embolectomy or insertion of an inferior, vena caval filter, intravenous fluid therapy, and drug therapy to increase cardiac output.

Position the patient for comfort; elevate head of bed to facilitate gas exchange, avoid bending at the knee.

Encourage patient to cough and take deep breathe to aid gas exchange and perfusion.

Avoid I.M. injections to decrease risk of Hematoma.

Provide a safe environment to prevent falls and injury to tissue.

Apply antiembolism stockings; remove them at night and put on again before the patient ambulates in the morning.

Teach the patient the important of preventing venous stasis by avoiding prolong standing or sitting and crossed legs.

In addition, if the patient have any question to please call her doctor.

Your doctor of healthcare provider determines how much coumadin you need to take by giving you a blood tests. The blood test is called a prothrombin time test, And is reported as an international normalized ratio (INR) Your dose might change so make sure you take the right dose of coumadin daily. And take your coumadin the same time every day and if you forget to take a pill tell you healthcare provider right away. Take the missed dose as soon as possible on the same day. And by no means do not take a double dose of coumadin to make up for the day you missed dose. At the begin you may have your blood tests every day for a few days, then one time a week. This will help your healthcare provide give you the dosage of coumadin that is right for you.

There are several things may change your PT/INR test results.

Such as sickness, diet, other medicines over the- counter. Or prescription, physical activities or your lifestyle.

Warfarin is used caution in older or debilitated person's to prevent bleeding.

A reduced dose to the elderly to prevent spontaneous intracranial bleeding or excessive bleeding related to trauma.

The older adults may have reduced liver or kidney function and decreased ability to metabolize and excrete Warfarin.

Wear a Medic/Alert bracelet or necklace and carry a Medic Alert card at all times.

Keep your eating habits and activities similar every day.

Do get your blood tested when you are suppose to.

Feel free to call your healthcare provide or your doctor, if you have any problems.

Possible Side Effects;

Check with your doctor as soon as possible if you experience diarrhea or any signs of illness, such as fever, *Contact you Doctor Immediately.*

If you experience any unusual pain, swelling, or discomfort, headache, dizziness, weakness, numberness, nose bleeding, or any excessive bleeding.

The patient should check for red or dark brown urine, red or tarry stools.

Check for purple, dark, purple toes syndrome. If any of these signs call, you doctor right away.

Drug Therapy

In patients at high risk for thromboembolism, minidose heparin therapy is recommend. A standard dose is usually 5000 units of heparin subcutaneously 2 hours preoperatively and then every 8 to 12 hours for 5 to 7 days.

Fibrinolytic Therapy

Fibrinolytic therapy is used to treat only massive pulmonary embolism. Therapy involves the use of thrombolytic enzymes streptokinase and urokinase. These drugs cause rapid lyses of large thrombi by activating plasminogen and converting it to plasmin.

Plasmin degrades fibrin clots, fibrinogen, and other plasma protein.

When fibrinolytic agents are use early, less than seven days, cause the clot to dissolve.

Restore normal circulation and hemodynamic change associated with embolization.

Prevent valve damage in deep veins.

Return normal blood flow patterns in the pulmonary vasculature.

Prevent pulmonary hypertension secondary to pulmonary emboli.

References

1. Albreachtsson, W., Anderson, J., and Einarsson, E. Streptokinase treatment of deep venous thrombosis and the post thrombotic syndrome, Arch Surg. 116:33, 1981

2. Bergman, D., Management of patient undergoing intraaortic ballon pump. Heart Lung . 3:916, 1974

3. Alderman, E. L., Brown, C. R., Sanders, G. R., et al, Survival following bypass graft surgery.45: 157, 1978

4. Dossey, B.M., et al, Critical Care Nursing: Body, Mind, and Spirit, 3rd ed. 1992

5. Greenfield, L. H. Steward, J. R., and Crute, S. Improved technique for insertion of Greenfield vena caval filter. Surg. Gynecology. Obstetric. 156:217, 1983.

6. Kathy A. Hausman, Donna D. Ignatavicius Medical Surgical 4th ed. 2002 Pgs. 577,646,

7. Sandra Smith Huddleston, RN, MSN, CCRN Critical Care and Emergency Nursing 2nd, ed. 1994

8. Mayor Clinic Family Health Book 3rd ed. 2003, 729,751, 752, 753,

10. New approaches to antithrombotic drugs. Nature 1991; 350(supply):30-33

11. Herbert JM, Herault JP, et al. Biochemical and pharmacological properties of SANORG 34006, a potent and long-acting synthetic pentasaccharide. Blood 1998; 91: 4197-4205 (PDR: 98, 99)

12. Tammy Chernin, RPh PDR, Monthly Prescribing GuidemVol.3 NO.1 January 2004 Pg. 100

About the Author

Mother, nurse, aspiring actress and author, Ashley Underwood is an American success story. The daughter of Southern sharecroppers, Ashley grew up in Eufaula, Alabama, during the turbulent '50s and understands the devastating effects of racial injustice. The fifth eldest child in a family of ten, she spent large amounts of time during her early years tending to the needs of her siblings and assisting her parents with chores on a 180-acre farm.

In those days, Ashley and her younger brothers constantly daydreamed about the adventures they would have and all the places they would travel to when they grew up. When she turned seventeen, Ashley moved to New Jersey to live with a relative, where one week later, she met her dream husband, Le'Von. Three years later, the couple was married.

She hit the real world with no idea of what kind of work she wanted to do. She tried everything, including working as a housekeeper in a nearby community medical center. A year later, she completed a nurse's assistant program. There, she found her life's passion and began her pursuit to finish her education and become a registered nurse.

In 1985, Ashley graduated with honors from the Middlesex County Nursing Program and in 1991; she graduated from Seton Hall University with a Bachelor's of Science in Nursing Degree.

Later, in 1995-1996, after two near-death experiences, she began writing her first novel, "The Eye Of An Angel." This Autobiographical novel discusses the presence of spiritual forces in our everyday lives.

Although she never intended to be an author, Mrs. Underwood believes that writing is a gift she received from God after her illness, and it has provided a wonderful challenge and is immensely satisfying. Mrs. Underwood currently resides in New Jersey with her loving husband, Le'Von, and the couples' faithful golden retriever, Dexter.